Best Outdoor Adventures
Near Minneapolis and Saint Paul

Help Us Keep This Guide Up to Date

Every effort has been made by the author and editors to make this guide as accurate and useful as possible. However, many things can change after a guide is published—trails are rerouted, Mother Nature alters terrain and waterways, regulations change, facilities come under new management, and so forth.

We welcome your comments concerning your experiences with this guide and how you feel it could be improved and kept up to date. While we may not be able to respond to all comments and suggestions, we'll take them to heart, and we'll also make certain to share them with the author. Please send your comments and suggestions to the following address:

FalconGuides
Reader Response/Editorial Department
246 Goose Lane
Guilford, CT 06437

Or you may e-mail us at:

editorial@falcon.com

Thanks for your input—now go out and have an adventure!

Best Outdoor Adventures Near
MINNEAPOLIS AND SAINT PAUL

A Guide to the Area's Greatest
Hiking, Paddling, and Cycling

JOE BAUR
CONTRIBUTIONS BY DAVID BAUR
AND STEVE JOHNSON

GUILFORD, CONNECTICUT

FALCONGUIDES®

An imprint of Globe Pequot
Falcon and FalconGuides are registered trademarks and Make Adventure Your Story is a trademark of Rowman & Littlefield.

Distributed by NATIONAL BOOK NETWORK

Maps by Melissa Baker and Alena Pearce © Rowman & Littlefield

Printed in the United States of America

British Library Cataloguing-in-Publication Information available

Library of Congress Cataloging-in-Publication Data available

ISBN 978-1-4930-1164-3 (paperback)
ISBN 978-1-4930-2878-8 (e-book)

∞™ The paper used in this publication meets the minimum requirements of American National Standard for Information Sciences—Permanence of Paper for Printed Library Materials, ANSI/NISO Z39.48-1992.

Contents

Overview

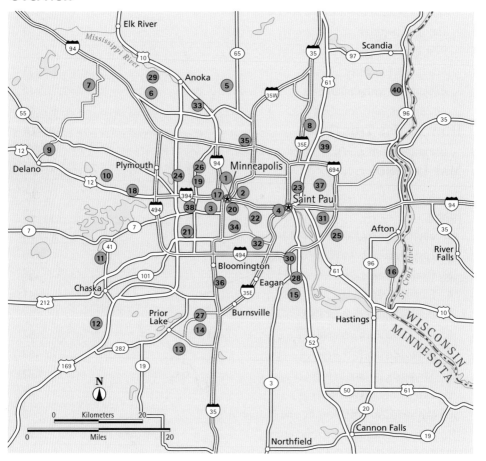

Acknowledgments

A sudden and serious injury sidelined me just a few weeks into the production of this book, putting the burden of the hikes squarely onto the shoulders of my brother David. In that spirit, math tells me I should only do a fraction of the acknowledgments. After all, I wouldn't want to take away in the slightest from his accomplishment.

In all seriousness, I have to start my acknowledgments just as my wise older brother did and as I did in my first book, *Best Hikes Near Cleveland*. This book, or any other project I partake in, would not be possible without the love, encouragement, and Mother Teresa–esque patience of my wife, Melanie. Scientists are still trying to figure out why she puts up with me and my never-ending battle with sitting still.

Of course I have to thank my brother for agreeing to partner with me on this book before I stabbed myself in some arteries with the handlebar of a mountain bike, requiring surgery and suddenly changing the terms of our original agreement. David did not hesitate to undertake the rest of this book on his own. If he did, he kept it from me or quite possibly vented to his significant other, Holly.

I'll go ahead and double down on all those my brother thanked. Aunt Barb, parents, and Holly, who I've taken to calling *cuñada*, because "sister-in-law" seems too damn formal for someone you've shared a bathroom with as long as we did when I moved to the Twin Cities for this book. I also want to thank Liz Pushing, an avid hiker in the area, who was kind enough to lead me on some of her favorite hikes in the region. Sara Woodruff of Silver Creek Paddle was invaluable in lending her expertise when it came to selecting paddles, as was Porter Million of the nonprofit Minnesota Off-Road Cyclists, who rode with me until the aforementioned stabbing of my arteries. Still, his insight made selecting the rides to include much easier. But because of that injury, I need to thank Steve Johnson, author of *Best Bike Rides Minneapolis and St. Paul* (FalconGuides), for agreeing to step in and lend a number of his favorite mountain-biking trails to this book. I'd also like to quickly thank One on One Bicycle Studio, Angry Catfish Bicycle, and the Freewheel Bike Midtown Bike Center for allowing me to try out a variety of bikes on the various rides and trails featured in the book.

Finally, there's you, the reader. Thank you for taking an interest in the trails, bike paths, and paddles of the Twin Cities. As a convert myself who happily considers the Twin Cities a second home, I know you will not be disappointed.

—Joe

Introduction

Weather

The Twin Cities of Minneapolis and Saint Paul are notorious for their brutally cold winters. However—and this may come as a surprise to some—there are three other distinct seasons throughout the year. Yes, winter is cold, with no shortage of the white stuff falling from the sky. But summers can be as pleasant as in San Diego, falls as colorful as the famous foliage of New England, and spring, well, it depends on the year. Unfortunately, climate change has brought on more extreme weather at both ends of the spectrum, as climate change is reported to do based on research by far more intelligent individuals than your authors. For now, the Twin Cities are still kicking and have yet to burst into flames or sink into any of the surrounding 10,000 lakes that Minnesota is so famous for. That means the Twin Cities are perfect for year-round hiking, cycling, and paddling until further notice!

Some new to the Twin Cities or visiting might be turned off by the winters. But move here or come for a weekend, and you'll quickly find that Minnesotans keep active no matter what Mother Nature throws at them. However, as can be expected, hiking, paddling, and cycling are most popular in the warmer, drier summer months. Even when the thermometer ticks up toward the upper 80s or even 90s, the worst of the heat can be avoided by doing your sport either early in the morning or in the evening hours. Plus you'll more often than not find shade in the surrounding greenery along these trails and paths, but do take caution when a paddle leaves you subject to an unobstructed sun.

Ultimately you'll want to consult your smartphone or your nearest weather-tracking technology before heading out on any long hike. Weather can change quickly in these parts, and even the predictions aren't foolproof. On the bright side, that means you have the opportunity to experience these hikes under a variety of weather conditions that will inevitably make for a different adventure each and every time.

Flora and Fauna

Flora

The story of Minneapolis and Saint Paul flora stretches back for hundreds of millions of years. Originally the area was covered in Saint Peter Sandstone underneath shale and limestone in the Ordovician period more than 400 million years ago. More recently—and we're still talking 20,000 years ago—the area known today as Minneapolis and Saint Paul was covered by the Superior Lobe of the Laurentide Ice Sheet. The Saint Croix moraine was left on the Twin Cities as the ice sheet receded. Over time, the Grantsburg Sublobe of the Des Moines Lobe took hold of the region as tunnels were formed beneath the thick layers of ice. This cut through the limestone and started releasing ice water. In its wake, troughs were left behind in the limestone and were filled by glacial sediment. When the sediment mixed with chunks of ice, it left voids in the soil and created basins for some of the more popular lakes of the Twin Cities, such as Calhoun and Harriet. This, of course, is merely a taste of the geological history that helped create the forests, wildflowers, wetlands, prairies, and tall grasses that give the area its natural beauty today.

Fauna

Thanks perhaps to the region's significant geological history, there's a diversity of fauna. Within the Minnesota Valley National Wildlife Refuge alone, you'll find wood ducks, river otters, and prairie skinks. There is no shortage of bird species, such as the barred owl, as well. Other wildlife you might come across includes beavers, deer, skunks, raccoons, and porcupines.

Wilderness Restrictions/Regulations

Minneapolis and Saint Paul run their parks a bit differently than other regions do. Whereas most readers might be used to an isolated park operated by, for example, the "XYZ Metroparks," a great number of the venues in this book are simply operated by the respective city's parks and recreation boards. These adventures and many more in the suburbs feature trails without a particular name. That's because the Twin Cities of Minneapolis and Saint Paul are essentially one giant interconnected park. Many of the urban-area hikes in the book, such as the Chain of Lakes, were created by the authors based on what we thought made sense when considering location and distance. Truth is, you could hike around Minneapolis and Saint Paul almost without touching a city sidewalk. The Twin Cities should be commended for this phenomenal commitment to green space, which provides locals and visitors alike with an incredible tapestry of trails to choose from. We marked trails, routes, and paddles based on what made sense to us, but other locals may have their own preferences. Over time, as you become better acquainted with the area, you might come up with your own favorite routes.

There are some other governing bodies of the trails in this book, such as the Three Rivers Park District, and they are noted within each chapter. Feel free to consult the respective managing body with any specific questions regarding regulations. Ultimately you'll find that the Twin Cities are hiking cities, and no regulation will keep you from enjoying this phenomenal region.

Getting Around Minneapolis and Saint Paul

Area Codes
The area codes in and surrounding the Twin Cities are 612, 952, 651, and 763.

Roads
The activities selected for this book were chosen because they are (with perhaps one or two exceptions) within a 45-minute drive of either Minneapolis or Saint Paul. Urbanites and tourists who tend to stay downtown will be pleased to know that the urban hikes are accessible by foot, bike, or public transit. This being the Twin Cities, many of the hikes are also accessible by bike or Nice Ride—the regional bike-share program. However, some activities either require or are best accessed by car. Outside of urban Minneapolis and Saint Paul, I-35, I-494, and I-94 will be your primary routes for these adventures.

By Air
Minneapolis–Saint Paul International Airport is located south and in between the Twin Cities along the Minnesota River, as well as some of the activities you'll be experiencing. The airport is accessible via the aforementioned highways, but the region's relatively young light-rail system is the best choice for connecting visitors with either downtown.

By Rail

Minneapolis and Saint Paul are served by Amtrak and Metro Transit.

By Bus

Greyhound and Megabus have stops in the respective downtown areas.

Visitor Information

For general information on Minneapolis and Saint Paul, visit Meet Minneapolis (minneapolis.org) and Visit Saint Paul (visitsaintpaul.com), respectively. Outside the Twin Cities, check Explore Minnesota (exploreminnesota.com).

The Ten Essentials

It's important to have a very healthy respect for Mother Nature. Conditions in the Twin Cities are notorious for changing rapidly and with little or no warning. The "expect the best, but prepare for the worst" adage is a great thing to keep in mind when you're preparing to go into the wilderness, or even just hiking in a city park. Always let somebody know where you're going and when you plan on being back. Know your limitations, and, as already stated, err on the side of caution. If conditions of any sort are making you uncomfortable, that's a good sign to head back or take appropriate action.

Be prepared. Whether you are new to the outdoors or an Eagle Scout, the ten essentials are something that all hikers should have on hand. Here is a list of the updated essential "systems" for hikers, but cyclists and paddlers should consider these as well, particularly items 1, 2, 3, and 9.

1. **Navigation.** A map and a compass are mandatory. These can be augmented with things like altimeters and GPS units, but always have a map of the area and a compass. Map suggestions/recommendations are included with many hiking and cycling descriptions.

2. **Sun protection.** Bring sunglasses, sunscreen, and proper clothing, including a hat.

3. **Insulation.** Will there be a blizzard in July? Probably not. However, you should have whatever it takes to survive the worst conditions that can be reasonably expected. No matter the season, start your outfit with wicking gear: clothing that is not made of cotton and that can wick moisture away

from the body. Dress in layers, especially in cooler weather. Pack extra socks. If things are going to be cold or wet, bring additional layers and rain gear. Whatever the conditions, avoid cotton.

4. **Illumination.** Flashlights, headlamps, and LEDs all work. It's good to have a backup light source or spare batteries.

5. **First-aid supplies.** It's up to you whether to bring such things as allergy pills or latex gloves. At the very least you will need some gauze, bandages, tape, and pain meds. There are many prepackaged kits available that include everything from bare-bones basics to an outdoor aid station.

6. **Fire.** This includes waterproof matches, disposable lighters, and chemical heat tabs.

7. **Repair kit and tools.** A knife or multi-tool is fairly standard. Depending on what you're doing, duct tape and rope can be handy as well.

8. **Nutrition.** Carry at least enough food for an extra day and night in the wilderness. Nutrition bars, jerky, nuts, and the like all work.

9. **Hydration.** Always bring at least a full water bottle or water bladder/reservoir system. You should also have some sort of water treatment or filtration on hand.

10. Emergency shelter. If you're backpacking, the tent you're carrying covers this one. If you're out for the day, consider a space blanket, rain gear, or even a trash bag.

First Aid

I know you're tough, but get 10 miles into the woods and develop a blister and you'll wish you had carried that first-aid kit. Face it; it's just plain good sense. Many companies produce lightweight, compact first-aid kits. Just make sure yours contains at least the following:

❑ adhesive bandages
❑ moleskin or duct tape
❑ sterile gauze and dressings in various sizes
❑ white surgical tape

- ❏ Ace bandage
- ❏ antihistamine
- ❏ aspirin
- ❏ Povidone-iodine solution, such as Betadine
- ❏ first-aid book
- ❏ antacid tablets
- ❏ tweezers
- ❏ scissors
- ❏ antibacterial wipes
- ❏ triple-antibiotic ointment
- ❏ plastic gloves
- ❏ sterile cotton-tip applicators
- ❏ syrup of ipecac (to induce vomiting)
- ❏ thermometer
- ❏ wire splint

Here are a few tips for dealing with, and hopefully preventing, certain ailments.

Sunburn. Take along sunscreen or sunblock, protective clothing, and a wide-brimmed hat. If you do get a sunburn, treat the area with aloe vera gel, and protect the area from further sun exposure. At higher elevations, the sun's radiation can be particularly damaging to skin. Remember that your eyes are vulnerable to this radiation as well. Sunglasses can be a good way to prevent headaches and permanent eye damage from the sun, especially in places where light-colored rock or patches of snow reflect light up into your face.

Blisters. Be prepared to take care of these hike spoilers by carrying moleskin (a lightly padded adhesive), gauze, and tape, or adhesive bandages. An effective way to apply moleskin is to cut out a circle of moleskin and remove the center—like a doughnut—and place it over the blistered area. Cutting the center out will reduce the pressure applied to the sensitive skin. Other products can help you combat blisters. Some are applied to suspicious hot spots before a blister forms to help decrease friction to that area, while others are applied to the blister after it has popped to help prevent further irritation.

Insect bites and stings. You can treat most insect bites and stings by applying 1 percent hydrocortisone cream topically and taking a pain medication such as ibuprofen. If you forgot to pack these items, a cold compress or a paste of mud and ashes can sometimes assuage the itching and discomfort. Remove any stingers by using tweezers or scraping the area with your fingernail or a knife blade. Don't pinch the area; you'll only spread the venom.

Some people are highly sensitive to bites and stings and may have a serious allergic reaction that can be life threatening. Symptoms of a serious allergic reaction can include wheezing, an asthmatic attack, and shock. The treatment for this severe type of reaction is epinephrine. If you know that you are sensitive to bites and stings, carry a prepackaged kit of epinephrine, which can be obtained only by prescription from your doctor.

Ticks. Ticks can carry diseases such as Rocky Mountain spotted fever and Lyme disease. The best defense is, of course, prevention. If you know you're going to be hiking through an area littered with ticks, wear long pants and a long-sleeved shirt. You can apply a permethrin-based repellent to your clothing and a DEET-based repellent to exposed skin. At the end of your hike, do a spot check for ticks. If you do find a tick, grab the head of the tick firmly—with a pair of tweezers if you have them—and gently pull it away from the skin with a twisting motion. Sometimes the mouth parts linger, embedded in your skin. If this happens, try to remove them with a disinfected needle. Clean the affected area with an antibacterial cleanser and then apply triple antibiotic ointment. Monitor the area for a few days. If irritation persists or a white spot or bull's-eye rash develops, see a doctor for possible infection.

Poison ivy, poison oak, and poison sumac. These skin irritants can be found most anywhere in North America and come in the form of a bush or a vine, having leaflets in groups of three, five, seven, or nine. Learn how to spot the plants. The oil they secrete can cause an allergic reaction in the form of blisters, usually about 12 hours after exposure. The itchy rash can last from ten days to several weeks. The best defense against these irritants is to wear clothing that covers the arms, legs, and torso. For summer, zip-off cargo pants come in handy. There are also nonprescription lotions you can apply to exposed skin that guard against the effects of poison ivy/oak/sumac and can be washed off with soap and water. Should you contract a rash from any of these plants, use an antihistamine to reduce the itching. If the rash is localized, create a light-bleach-and-water wash to dry up the area. If the rash has spread, either tough it out or see your doctor about getting a dose of cortisone (available both orally and by injection).

Snakebites. Snakebites are rare in North America. Unless startled or provoked, the majority of snakes will not bite. If you are wise to their habitats and keep a careful eye on the trail, you should be just fine. When stepping over logs, first step on the log, making sure you can see what's on the other side before stepping down. Though your chances of being struck are slim, it's wise to know what to do in the event you are.

If a *nonvenomous* snake bites you, allow the wound to bleed a small amount and then cleanse the wounded area with a 10 percent povidone-iodine solution (Betadine). Rinse the wound with clean water (preferably) or fresh urine (it might sound repulsive, but it's sterile). Once the area is clean, cover it with triple antibiotic ointment and a clean bandage. Remember, most residual damage from snakebites, venomous or otherwise, comes from infection rather than the bite itself. Keep the area as clean as possible and get medical attention immediately.

If somebody in your party is bitten by a venomous snake, follow these steps:

1. Calm the victim.

2. Remove jewelry, watches, and restrictive clothing, and immobilize the affected limb. Do not elevate the injury. Medical opinions vary on whether the area should be lower or level with the heart, but the consensus is that it should not be above it.

3. Make a note of the circumference of the limb at the bite site and at various points above the site as well. This will help you monitor swelling.

4. Evacuate the victim. Ideally he should be carried out to minimize movement. If the victim appears to be doing okay, he can walk. Stop and rest frequently. If the swelling appears to be spreading or the victim's symptoms increase, change your plan and find a way to transport him.

5. If you are waiting for rescue, make sure to keep the victim comfortable and hydrated (unless he begins vomiting).

Snakebite treatment is rife with out-of-date and potentially dangerous remedies: You used to be told to cut the bite site and suck the venom out or use a suction-cup extractor for the same purpose; applying an electric shock to the area was even in vogue for a while. Do *not* do any of these things. Do not apply ice, do not give the victim painkillers, and do not apply a tourniquet. All you really want to do is keep the victim calm and get help. If you're alone and have to seek help, don't run—you'll only increase the flow of blood—and venom—throughout your system. Instead, remain calm.

Dehydration. Have you ever exerted yourself in hot weather and had a roaring headache and felt fatigued after only a few miles? More than likely you were dehydrated. Symptoms of dehydration include fatigue, headache, and decreased coordination and judgment. When you are hiking, your body's rate of fluid loss depends on a number of factors, including outside temperature, humidity, altitude, and your activity level. On average, a hiker walking in warm weather will lose 4 liters of fluid a day. That fluid loss is easily replaced by normal consumption of liquids and food. However, hikers walking briskly in hot, dry weather and hauling a heavy pack can lose 1 to 3 liters of water an hour. It's important to always carry plenty of water and to stop often and drink fluids regularly, even if you aren't thirsty. The same is true for cyclists and paddlers.

Heat exhaustion is the result of a loss of large amounts of electrolytes and often occurs if one is dehydrated and has been under heavy exertion. Common symptoms of heat exhaustion include cramping, exhaustion, fatigue, lightheadedness, and nausea. You can treat heat exhaustion by getting out of the sun and drinking an electrolyte solution made up of 1 teaspoon of salt and 1 tablespoon of sugar dissolved in 1 liter of water. Drink this solution slowly over a period of 1 hour. Drinking plenty of fluids (preferably an electrolyte solution or sports drink) can prevent heat exhaustion. Avoid outdoor activities during the hottest parts of the day, and wear breathable clothing, a wide-brimmed hat, and sunglasses.

Hypothermia is one of the biggest dangers for outdoors enthusiasts in the summertime. That may sound strange, but imagine starting out on a hike/ride/paddle in midsummer when it's sunny and 80°F out. You're clad in nylon shorts and a cotton T-shirt. About halfway through your route, the sky begins to cloud up; in the next hour a light drizzle begins to fall, and the wind starts to pick up. Before you know it you are soaking wet and shivering—the perfect recipe for hypothermia. More-advanced symptoms include decreased coordination, slurred speech, and blurred vision. When a victim's temperature falls below 92°F, blood pressure and pulse plummet, possibly leading to coma and death.

To avoid hypothermia, always bring layers of clothing, gloves, and a hat. Learn to adjust your layers based on the temperature. If you are proceeding at a moderate pace, you will stay warm; but when you stop for a break you'll become cold quickly, unless you add more layers of clothing.

If someone is showing advanced signs of hypothermia, dress her in dry clothes and make sure she is wearing a hat and gloves. Place the person in a sleeping bag in a tent or shelter that will protect her from the wind and other elements. Give the person warm fluids to drink, and keep her awake.

Frostbite. When the mercury dips below 32°F, your extremities begin to chill. If a persistent chill attacks a localized area, say, your hands or your toes, the circulatory system reacts by cutting off blood flow to the affected area—the idea being to protect and preserve the body's overall temperature. And so it's death by attrition for the affected area. Ice crystals start to form from the water in the cells of the neglected tissue. Deprived of heat, nourishment, and now water, the tissue literally starves. This is frostbite.

Prevention is your best defense against this situation. Your face, hands, and feet are most prone to frostbite, so protect these areas well. Wool is the traditional material of choice because it provides ample airspace for insulation and draws moisture away from the skin. Synthetic fabrics, however, have made great strides in the cold-weather clothing market. Do your research. Wearing a pair of light silk liners under your regular gloves is a good trick for keeping warm. They afford some additional warmth, but more important, they'll allow you to remove your gloves for dexterous work without exposing the skin.

If your feet or hands start to feel cold or numb due to the elements, warm them as quickly as possible. Place cold hands under your armpits or bury them in your crotch. If your feet are cold, change your socks. If there's plenty of room in your shoes or boots, add another pair of socks. Do remember, though, that constricting your feet in tight footwear can restrict blood flow and actually make your feet colder more quickly. Your socks need to have breathing room if they're going to be effective. Dead air provides insulation. If your face is cold, place your warm hands over your face, or simply wear a head stocking.

Should your skin go numb and start to appear white and waxy, chances are you've got or are developing frostbite. Don't try to thaw the area unless you can maintain the warmth. In other words, don't stop to warm up your frostbitten feet only to head back on the trail. You'll do more damage than good. Tests have shown that people who continued on thawed feet did more harm, and endured more pain, than those who left the affected areas alone. Do your best to get out of the cold entirely and seek medical attention—which usually consists of performing a rapid rewarming in water for 20 to 30 minutes.

The overall objective in preventing both hypothermia and frostbite is to keep the body's core warm. Protect key areas where heat escapes, such as the top of the head, and maintain the proper nutrition level. Foods that are high in calories aid the body in producing heat. Never smoke or drink alcohol when you're in situations where the cold is threatening. By affecting blood flow, these activities ultimately cool the body's core temperature.

Hantavirus pulmonary syndrome (HPS). Deer mice spread the virus that causes HPS, and humans contract it from breathing it in, usually when they've disturbed an area with dust and mice feces from nests or surfaces with mice droppings or urine. Exposure to large numbers of rodents and their feces or urine presents the greatest risk. On your route, you may enter old buildings, and often deer mice live in these places. We may not be around long enough to be exposed, but do be aware of this disease. About half the people who develop HPS die. Symptoms are flulike and appear about two to three weeks after exposure. After initial symptoms, a dry cough and shortness of breath follow. Breathing is difficult. If you even think you might have HPS, see a doctor immediately!

Adventure Etiquette

Leave no trace. Always leave an area just as you found it—if not better than you found it. Avoid camping in fragile, alpine meadows and along the banks of streams and lakes. Use a camp stove versus building a wood fire. Pack out all your trash and extra food. Bury human waste at least 100 feet from water sources under 6 to 8 inches of topsoil. Don't bathe with soap in a lake or stream—use prepackaged moistened towelettes to wipe off sweat and dirt, or bathe in the water without soap. For more information visit LNT.org.

Stay on the trail. It's true, a path anywhere leads nowhere new, but purists will just have to get over it. Paths serve an important purpose: They limit impact on natural areas. Straying from a designated trail may seem innocent, but it can cause damage to sensitive areas—damage that may take years to recover, if it can recover at all. Even simple shortcuts can be destructive. So, please, stay on the trail.

Leave no weeds. Noxious weeds tend to overtake other plants, which in turn affects animals and birds that depend on those plants for food. To minimize the spread of noxious weeds, hikers and cyclists should regularly clean their boots, tents, packs, and hiking poles of mud and seeds. Also brush your dog to remove any weed seeds before heading off into a new area. Paddlers should clean oars and boats to avoid the transference of plant material.

Keep your dog under control. You can buy a flexi-lead that allows your dog to go exploring along the trail, while allowing you the ability to reel him in should another hiker or cyclist approach or should he decide to chase a rabbit. Always obey leash laws, and be sure to bury your dog's waste or pack it out in resealable plastic bags.

Respect fellow travelers. Often you're not the only one on the trail or in the water. If you're on a multiuse trail, assume the appropriate precautions. When you encounter motorized vehicles (ATVs, motorcycles, and 4WDs), be alert. Though they should always yield to the hiker or bicyclist, often they're going too fast or are too lost in the buzz of their engine to react to your presence. If you hear activity ahead, step off the trail just to be safe. When hiking, note that you're not likely to hear a mountain biker coming, so be prepared and know ahead of time whether you share the trail with them. Cyclists should always yield to hikers. Be aware. When you approach horses or pack animals on the trail, always step quietly off the trail, preferably on the downhill side, and let them pass. To some animals, a hiker wearing a large backpack might appear threatening, so it's often a good idea to sit down. Make sure your dog doesn't harass these animals, and respect ranchers' rights while you're enjoying yours.

Adventures with Children

Hiking, cycling, or paddling with children isn't a matter of how many miles you can cover or how fast; it's about seeing and experiencing nature through their eyes.

Kids like to explore and have fun. They like to stop and point out bugs and plants, look under rocks, watch for fish or turtles, and throw sticks. If you're taking a toddler or young child on a hike, start with a trail you're familiar with. Trails that have interesting things for kids, like piles of leaves to play in or a small stream to wade through during the summer, will make the hike much more enjoyable for them and will keep them from getting bored. For early bike or boat trips, the advice is similar. Start with a short, familiar route, hopefully with interesting things to see along the way. And don't forget the safety equipment: bike helmets and PFDs (personal flotation devices) are a must.

You can keep your child's attention if you have a strategy before starting out. Using games is not only an effective way to keep a child's attention but also a great way to teach him or her about nature. Quiz children on the names of plants and animals. Pick up a family-friendly outdoor hobby like geocaching (geocaching.com) or letterboxing (atlasquest.com), both of which combine the outdoors, clue solving, and treasure hunting and can be done by foot, by bike, or by boat. If your children are old enough, let them carry or stow their own daypack filled with snacks and water. So that you are sure to go at their pace and not yours, let them lead the way on a hike or bike ride. Playing follow the leader works particularly well when you have a group of children. Have each child take a turn at being the leader.

With children, bringing a lot of clothing, regardless of the season, is key. The only thing predictable about weather is that it will change. In winter have your children wear wool socks and warm layers, such as long underwear, a fleece jacket and hat, wool mittens, and good rain gear. It's not a bad idea to have these along in late fall and early spring as well. For hiking, good footwear is also important. A sturdy pair of high-top tennis shoes or lightweight hiking boots is the best bet for little ones. In summer near a lake or stream, bring along a pair of old sneakers that your child can put on to go exploring in the water. Remember when you're near any type of water, always watch your child at all times. Also, keep a close eye on teething toddlers, who may decide a rock or leaf of poison oak is an interesting item to put in their mouth.

From spring through fall, you'll want your kids to wear a wide-brimmed hat to keep their face, head, and ears protected from the hot sun. Also, make sure your children wear sunscreen at all times. Choose a brand without PABA (para-aminobenzoic acid)—children have sensitive skin and may have an allergic reaction to sunscreen that contains it. If your child is younger than 6 months, don't use sunscreen or insect repellent. Instead, be sure his or her head, face, neck, and ears are protected from the sun with a wide-brimmed hat, and that all other skin exposed to the sun is protected with the appropriate clothing.

Remember that food is fun. Kids like snacks, so it's important to bring a lot of munchies for the trail. Stopping often for snack breaks is a fun way to keep the activity interesting. Raisins, apples, granola bars, crackers and cheese, cereal, and trail mix all make great snacks. Also, a few of their favorite candy treats can go a long way toward heading off a fit of fussing. If your children are old enough to carry their own backpacks, let them carry some lightweight "comfort" items, such as a doll, a small stuffed animal, or a little toy (you'll have to draw the line at bringing the 10-pound Tonka truck). If your kids don't like drinking water, you can bring some powdered drink mix or a juice box.

When hiking, be sure your child carrier is well designed—you don't want to break your back carrying your child. Most carriers designed to hold a 40-pound child will contain a large pocket to hold diapers and other items. Some have an optional rain/sun hood.

Adventures with Your Dog

Bringing your furry friend with you is always more fun than leaving him behind. Our canine pals make great buddies because they never complain and always make good company. Hiking, cycling, or paddling with your dog can be a rewarding experience, especially if you plan ahead.

Getting your dog in shape. Before you plan outdoor adventures with your dog, make sure he or she is in shape for the outing. Getting your dog into shape takes the same discipline as getting yourself into shape; luckily, your dog can get in shape with you. Take your dog with you on your daily runs or walks. If there is a park near your house, hit a tennis ball or play Frisbee with your dog.

Swimming is also an excellent way to get your dog into shape. If your dog likes the water, have her retrieve a tennis ball or stick. Gradually build your dog's stamina up over a two- to three-month period. A good rule of thumb is to assume that your dog will travel twice as far as you will on the trail or route. If you plan on doing a 5-mile hike, ride, or paddle, be sure your dog is in shape for a 10-mile distance.

Training your dog for adventure. Before you go on your first adventure with your dog, be sure he has a firm grasp on the basics of canine etiquette and behavior. Make sure he can sit, lie down, stay, and come. One of the most important commands you can teach your canine pal is to "come" under any situation. It's easy for your friend's nose to lead him astray or possibly get him lost. Another helpful command is the "get behind" command. When you're on a narrow path, you can have your dog follow behind you when other trail users approach. Nothing is more bothersome than an enthusiastic dog that runs back and forth on the trail and disrupts the peace of the trail for others—or, worse, jumps up on others and gets them muddy. When you see others approaching you on the trail or water, give them the right of way by quietly moving aside and making your dog lie down or stay in the boat until they pass.

Equipment. Whatever your mode of transport, the most critical pieces of equipment you can invest in for your dog are proper identification and a sturdy leash. Flexi-leads work well for hiking because they give your dog more freedom to explore but still leave you in control. For cycling, use a nontangling lead and a body harness. Make sure your dog has identification that includes your name and address and a number for your veterinarian. Other forms of identification for your dog include a tattoo or a microchip. You should consult your veterinarian for more information on these last two options.

The next piece of equipment you'll want to consider is a pack for your dog. By no means should you hold all of your dog's essentials in your pack—let her carry her own gear! Dogs that are in good shape can carry 30 to 40 percent of their own weight. Or if you're paddling, stow the gear in the bottom of the boat.

Most packs are fitted by a dog's weight and girth measurement. Companies that make dog packs generally include guidelines to help you pick out the size that's right for your dog. Some characteristics to look for when purchasing a pack for your dog include a harness that contains two padded girth straps, a padded chest strap, leash attachments, removable saddle bags, internal water bladders, and external gear cords.

You can introduce your dog to the pack by first placing the empty pack on his back and letting him wear it around the yard. Keep an eye on your furry friend during this first introduction. He may decide to chew through the straps if you aren't watching him closely. Once he learns to treat the pack as an object of fun and not a foreign enemy, fill the pack evenly on both sides with a few ounces of dog food in resealable plastic bags. Have your dog wear his pack on your daily walks for a period of two to three weeks. Each week add a little more weight to the pack until your dog will accept carrying the maximum amount of weight he can carry.

You can also purchase collapsible water and dog food bowls for your dog. These bowls are lightweight and can easily be stashed into your pack or your dog's. If you are hiking or biking on rocky terrain or in the snow, you can purchase footwear for your dog that will protect her feet from cuts and bruises.

Always carry plastic bags to remove feces from the trail. It is a courtesy to other trail users and helps protect local wildlife.

The following is a list of items to bring when you take your dog on an adventure:

- ❏ collapsible water bowls
- ❏ comb
- ❏ collar/harness and leash
- ❏ dog food and/or snacks
- ❏ plastic bags for feces
- ❏ a dog pack
- ❏ flea and tick powder
- ❏ a life jacket

- ❏ paw protection
- ❏ water
- ❏ a first-aid kit that contains eye ointment, tweezers, scissors, stretchy foot wrap, gauze, antibacterial wash, sterile cotton-tip applicators, antibiotic ointment, and cotton wrap

First aid for your dog. Your dog is just as prone—if not more prone—to getting in trouble on the trail or water as you are, so be prepared. Here's a rundown of the more likely misfortunes that might befall your little friend.

Bees and wasps. If a bee or wasp stings your dog, remove the stinger with a pair of tweezers and place a mudpack or a cloth dipped in cold water over the affected area.

Porcupines. One good reason to keep your dog on a leash is to prevent him from getting a nose full of porcupine quills. You may be able to remove the quills with pliers, but a veterinarian is the best person to do this nasty job because most dogs need to be sedated.

Heat stroke. Avoid hiking with your dog in really hot weather. Dogs with heat stroke will pant excessively, lie down and refuse to get up, and become lethargic and disoriented. If your dog shows any of these signs, have her lie down in the shade. If you are near a stream, pour cool water over your dog's entire body to help bring her body temperature back to normal.

Heartworm. Dogs get heartworms from mosquitoes, which carry the disease in the prime mosquito months of July and August. Giving your dog a monthly pill prescribed by your veterinarian easily prevents this condition.

Plant pitfalls. One of the biggest plant hazards for dogs on the trail are foxtails. Foxtails are pointed grass seed heads that bury themselves in your friend's fur, between his toes, and even get in his ear canal. If left unattended, these nasty seeds can work their way under the skin and cause abscesses and other problems. If you have a long-haired dog, consider trimming the hair between the toes and giving him a summer haircut to help prevent foxtails from attaching to his fur. After every hike, always look over your dog for these seeds—especially between his toes and in his ears.

Other plant hazards include burrs, thorns, thistles, and poison oak. If you find any burrs or thistles on your dog, remove them as soon as possible, before they become an unmanageable mat. Thorns can pierce a dog's foot and cause a great deal of pain. If you see that your dog is lame, stop and check his paws for thorns. Dogs are immune to poison oak, but they can pick up the sticky, oily substance from the plant and transfer it to you.

Protect those paws. Be sure to keep your dog's nails trimmed to avoid getting soft tissue or joint injuries. If your dog slows and refuses to go on, check to see that her paws aren't torn or worn. You can protect your dog's paws from trail hazards such as sharp gravel, foxtails, lava scree, and thorns by purchasing dog boots.

Sunburn. If your dog has light skin, he is an easy target for sunburn on his nose and other exposed skin areas. You can apply a nontoxic sunscreen—one without zinc oxide—to exposed skin areas that will help protect him from overexposure to the sun.

Ticks and fleas. Ticks can easily give your dog Lyme disease, as well as other diseases. Before you hit the trail, treat your dog with a flea-and-tick spray or powder. You can also ask your veterinarian about a once-a-month topical treatment that repels fleas and ticks.

Mosquitoes and deerflies. These little flying machines can do a job on your dog's snout and ears. Spraying your dog with fly repellent for horses will discourage both pests.

Giardia. Dogs can get giardia, which results in diarrhea. It is usually not debilitating, but it's definitely messy. A vaccine against giardia is available.

Mushrooms. Make sure your dog doesn't sample mushrooms along the trail. They could be poisonous to her, but she doesn't know that.

When you are finally ready to head out with your dog, keep in mind that national parks and many wilderness areas do not allow dogs. Always call ahead to see what the restrictions are.

How to Use This Guide

This guide contains just about everything you'll ever need to choose, plan for, enjoy, and survive a hike, bike ride, or paddle near Minneapolis and Saint Paul. Stuffed with useful Twin Cities–area information, *Best Outdoor Adventures Near Minneapolis and Saint Paul* features forty mapped and cued adventures. Here's an outline of the book's major components:

Each section begins with an **introduction to the adventure** in which you're given a sweeping look at what lies ahead. Each adventure then starts with a short **summary** of the adventure's highlights. These quick overviews give you a taste of the adventures to follow.

Following the overview you'll find the **specs** relevant to the activity: quick, nitty-gritty details of the route. Most are self-explanatory, but here are some details:

Distance: This is the total distance of the recommended route.

Estimated time: This is the average time it will take to cover the route. It is based on the total distance and elevation gain of the trail and condition and difficulty of the water surface. Your fitness level will also affect your time.

Difficulty: Each adventure has been assigned a level of difficulty. The rating system was developed from several sources and personal experience. These levels are meant to be a guideline only. A particular adventure may prove easier or harder for different people depending on ability and physical fitness.

Trail surface: Here's general information about what to expect underfoot.

Seasons: You'll find general information on the best time of year to for your activity.

Other trail users: In addition to hikers, you may encounter equestrians, mountain bikers, in-line skaters, motor boats, and others.

Canine compatibility: Know the regulations before you take your dog with you. Dogs are not allowed on several trails in this book, and some waterways may not be hospitable.

Land status: This will let you know if the property is national forest, county open space, national park wilderness, and so on.

Fees and permits: You may need to carry money with you for park entrance fees and permits.

Trail contacts and maps: For hikes, the phone number and website URL are provided for the local land manager in charge of all the trails within the selected hike. Park and reserve websites often contain more-detailed maps to supplement the maps in this book and may show more recent trails. Before you head out, get trail access information, or contact the land manager after your visit if you see problems with trail erosion, damage, or misuse.

Other: This includes additional information that will enhance your adventure.

Finding the trailhead: Dependable driving directions to where you'll want to park.

The Hike, The Ride, or **The Paddle:** The meat of the chapter, this is detailed and honest, a carefully researched impression of the route. It also often includes area history, both natural and human.

Miles and Directions: For hiking and biking mileage cues identify all turns and trail name changes, as well as points of interest.

Options are provided for many entries to make your journey shorter or longer, depending on the amount of time you have.

The **Information** section provides material on local events and attractions, restaurants, tours, organizations, and other pertinent information.

Cycling, mountain biking, and paddling entries use different, more relevant criteria such as (Traffic) Hazards, River type, Current, Boats used, and the like.

Don't feel restricted to the routes and trails that are mapped here. Be adventurous; use this guide as a platform to discover new routes for yourself. One of the simplest ways to begin is to just turn the map upside down and conquer any route in reverse. The change in perspective is often fantastic, and the adventure should feel quite different. It'll be like getting two distinctly different adventures on each map. For your own purposes, you may wish to copy the route directions onto a small sheet of paper to help you while outside or photocopy the map and cue sheet to take with you. Otherwise, just slip this book in your backpack and take it all with you. Enjoy your time in the outdoors, and remember to pack out what you pack in.

Using the Maps

Overview map: This map shows the location of each hike in the area by hike number.

Route map: This is your primary guide to each featured route. It shows many accessible roads and trails, points of interest, water, landmarks, and geographical features. It also distinguishes trails from roads and paved roads from unpaved roads. The selected route is highlighted, and directional arrows point the way.

Map Legend

Municipal

═╬═ (494)	Interstate Highway
═(12)═	Featured US Highway
═(12)═	US Highway
═(101)═	Featured State Road
═(101)═	State Road
═(16)═	Featured County/Local Road
═(16)═	County/Local Road
═ ═ ═ ═	Gravel Road
═ ═ ═ ═	Unpaved Road
├──┼──┤	Railroad
─ ─ · ─ · ─	State Boundary

Trails

━━━━	Featured Paved Trail
────	Paved Trail
▬▬▬▬	Featured Trail
- - - - -	Trail
- - - - -	Paddle Route

Water Features

⬭	Body of Water
⟋⟍	Marsh
∿	River/Creek
≋	Waterfall

Symbols

⦀⦀⦀	Boardwalk
⏝⏝	Bridge
■	Building/Point of Interest
▲	Campground
◄—	Mileage Marker
🅿	Parking
⊞	Picnic Area
🍴	Restaurant
🚻	Restrooms
⚐	Ski Area
○	Town
①	Trailhead
①	Trail Marker Number
❓	Visitor/Information Center

Land Management

▣	National Wildlife Refuge
▣	State/County/City Park
⌐ ¬	National Reserve/Nature Center

Looking back toward the city along the East River Flats. DAVID BAUR

HIKING

Hiking is inarguably the most accessible form of adventure. As soon as you walk out of your home, you can be on a hike. This is especially true in the Twin Cities, where great care has been taken to ensure city residents can still get a healthy dose of greenery without having to shack up in a cabin or campground. This is Minnesota we're talking about, however, so getting way out there into the thick of it is certainly an option as well.

Here we present a collection of our favorite hikes from *Best Hikes Near Minneapolis and Saint Paul*, including a number of urban hikes that allow you to get your heart pumping without leaving the city, some on the fringes of the Twin Cities with dirt trails crisscrossing through regional parks, and even a few that will send you through the remote rivers and streams of the ever-popular Minnesotan forests. Come winter, you can throw on a pair of snowshoes to keep the adventure going, or maybe even strap on some cross-country skis.

It's hard to mistake these directions as the wood-chip trail leads into the forest. DAVID BAUR

1 Saint Anthony Falls Heritage Trail

This hike is a study in contrasts. You'll walk through parklands and trails, alongside the Mississippi River, and amid the trees, but you will also be surrounded by the Minneapolis skyline and some important parts of the city's industrial history. You'll experience parts of the city that are critical for understanding its past, while strolling through some of today's fastest growing neighborhoods. It's rare for a hike to feature both beautiful architecture and a natural wonder like the Mississippi River, but this hike brings them together.

Start: Intersection of East Island Avenue and Merriam Street on Nicollet Island in Minneapolis

Distance: 3.8-mile loop with side trails

Hiking time: About 1.5 hours

Difficulty: Easy

Trail surface: Mostly blacktop trails except for brief segments of dirt trails in Water Power Park and on the Lower Trail

Best season: Year-round

Other trail users: Cyclists

Canine compatibility: Leashed dogs permitted

Land status: Public land, city parks

Fees and permits: No fees or permits required

Schedule: N/A for city streets; 6 a.m. to 10 p.m. daily within park spaces

Trail contacts and maps: Minneapolis Park & Recreation Board; (612) 230-6400; minneapolisparks.org

Finding the trailhead: From I-35 W, exit onto 4th Street SE, heading west. After approximately 0.8 mile, turn left onto 1st Avenue NE and head southwest for about 0.2 mile. Turn left onto SE Main Street just before 1st Avenue NE crosses the river via the Hennepin Avenue Bridge. At the first intersection, turn right onto Merriam Street. After crossing the Merriam Street Bridge, look for any available parking spot not reserved for the Nicollet Island Inn. The trailhead is on the eastern side of Merriam Street, at the intersection with East Island Avenue. GPS: N44°59.14333' / W93°15.59500'

The Hike

Depending on whether you arrive via bike, public transit, or car, where you truly begin your hike can change a bit. For our purposes, the hike begins on the east side of Nicollet Island, where you'll pick up the trail on the east side of Merriam Street just before the Merriam Street Bridge. Look for the information stand with some of the island's history and a map to help you get your bearings before heading northeast across the Merriam Street Bridge toward Main Street. Changes in the trail are generally well marked using green signs with white lettering. The first of these is just across the bridge and will direct you to a right-hand turn (southeast) to follow the Saint Anthony Falls Heritage Trail.

After a few minutes strolling near Main Street, an opening in the fence invites you into Water Power Park. This optional point of interest offers great views of the falls and the chance to experience the power of the river up close and to learn about the history of milling and electricity generation at Saint Anthony Falls. That last part is a good deal more interesting than it may sound and makes the trek worthwhile.

Farther along Main Street you'll pass the Pillsbury A-Mill building. Once the largest flour mill in the world, it is now a protected historic landmark that has been restored and renovated into artists' lofts. Across the street from the

Peeking through the trees for a view of the Stone Arch Bridge over the Mississippi River. HOLLY BAUR

FESTIVALS ON MAIN STREET

Minneapolis's historic Main Street is a hive of activity any time of year, but three major events stand out.

In spring the Saint Anthony Main Theatre Complex plays host to the Minneapolis–Saint Paul International Film Festival. The largest film festival in the Upper Midwest, it draws more than 40,000 annual attendees.

On Father's Day weekend, the Stone Arch Bridge Festival draws hundreds of artists, food vendors, and musicians. Concerts begin on the Wednesday prior to the weekend, while the main art festival is on Saturday and Sunday.

The Northern Spark Festival, a one-night-only art festival, begins around sunset on the second Saturday in June and runs into sunrise the following morning. Technically this festival changes featured locations year to year, but some part of the Saint Anthony Main and Mill District area always seems to make the cut, given the importance of the Mississippi River to the city and the area's unique architecture.

Pillsbury building, another sign points you down to the Lower Trail. As you descend the stairs and make your way along the path at the bottom, look for a break in the foliage back against the cliff side. You should be able to spot a door, now attached to nothing at all, that once led into the bowels of the mill above. While exploring the area along the river, you will eventually reach a sort of bridge to nowhere. This part of the trail may be a dead end, but it provides some great views of the Stone Arch Bridge, which is where you're headed next.

The Stone Arch Bridge is an immensely popular attraction in Minneapolis, and if you're hiking on a Saturday, there's a pretty good chance you'll see a wedding party or three taking photos. Heading southwest across the bridge affords some spectacular views of downtown and the falls. There's no shame in stopping for your own photo op.

As you exit the bridge, take a sharp left to head down the paved ramp to and underneath the bridge alongside the Saint Anthony Falls Lock and Dam. This area is known as Mill Ruins Park, the reasons for which are pretty obvious. The remnants of old mill buildings give you a vision of Minneapolis's past as one of the grain capitals of the world. The nearby hillside is filled with wildflowers in summer, offering a contrast to the ramshackle ruins.

Heading back toward Nicollet Island, you come to Father Louis Hennepin Bridge, named for the Catholic priest and explorer who made the European discovery of Saint Anthony Falls. First Bridge Park underneath the bridge also commemorates the spot, recognizing a previous structure as the location of the first permanent bridge across the Mississippi. Walking the bridge, you'll get up-close views of the regionally famous Grain Belt sign, named for an old local brewery just a couple of miles away. Back on Nicollet Island, keep an eye out for the *Bell of Two Friends* sculpture, a gift from Minneapolis's sister city, Ibaraki, Japan, before wrapping up your hike alongside the Nicollet Island Inn.

These green signs with white lettering help you stick to the trail in the midst of all the action along Main Street. HOLLY BAUR

Miles and Directions

0.0 Start at Merriam Street and East Island Avenue. Hike east across the Merriam Street Bridge toward SE Main Street and turn right (southeast) onto the Saint Anthony Falls Heritage Trail.

0.4 Turn right (south) off the Saint Anthony Falls Heritage Trail into Water Power Park.

0.5 Turn right again (west) into the main area of Water Power Park. Follow the dirt trail out to a viewing area to see the falls before retracing your steps back out to the Saint Anthony Falls Heritage Trail.

0.8 Turn right, back onto the Saint Anthony Falls Heritage Trail (southeast) toward SE 3rd Avenue.

0.9 Shortly after crossing SE 3rd Avenue, turn right (south) to head down the stairs, marked by the green-and-white sign that reads Lower Trail.

1.0 Take the fork in the trail to head south; then turn left to walk down to the riverside before retracing your steps to the fork in the trail.

1.1 Back at the fork, turn right (southeast) and follow the trail for approximately 0.2 mile to a dead end on an elevated boardwalk.

Saint Anthony Falls Heritage Trail

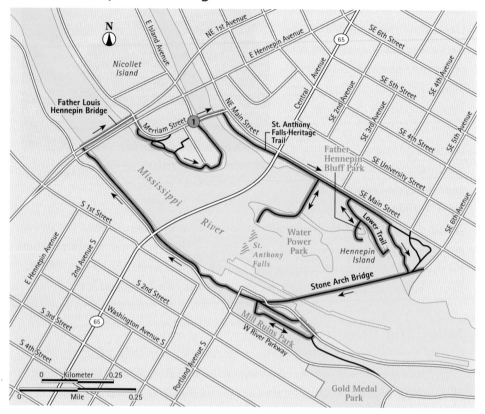

1.4   Turn right, back on to the Saint Anthony Falls Heritage Trail. Head southeast.

1.5   Veer right when the trail splits as it enters Father Hennepin Bluff Park.

1.6   Turn right (west) onto the Stone Arch Bridge.

2.1   At the end of the bridge, take a sharp left, followed by another immediate left to follow the concrete ramp downhill. Turn right to proceed underneath the bridge.

2.2   Cross Portland Avenue within the parking lot for the Saint Anthony Lock and Dam by heading southeast.

2.3   Turn right (south) and take the small flight of steps before turning right again (west) onto the metal boardwalk.

2.5   Follow the sidewalk to retrace your steps back up to the Stone Arch Bridge.

2.8   At the southwestern edge of the Stone Arch Bridge, pick up the trail as it continues off the bridge heading northwest. The trail wraps around the northern edge of the parking lot, with the Mississippi River on your right-hand side, before continuing upriver.

3.3 Take the staircase that leads up to the bridge deck and begin crossing the bridge, heading northeast. There is a staircase on each side of the bridge.

3.5 Take the stairs that lead below the bridge onto Nicollet Island. At the base of the stairs, turn left (southeast) on the blacktop trail.

3.6 Continue southeast, going counterclockwise around the east side of Nicollet Island at the *Bell of Two Friends* sculpture.

3.8 Arrive back at the trailhead.

Hike Information

Local Information: Meet Minneapolis; (612) 767-8000; minneapolis.org

Local Events and Attractions: Minneapolis–Saint Paul International Film Festival; mspfilm .org/festivals/mspiff/

Northern Spark; arts festival; June; northernspark.org

Stone Arch Bridge Festival; weekend of art and music; June; stonearchbridgefestival .com

Hike Tours: Magical History Tour; magicalhistorytour.com

2 East River Flats to Witch's Hat

East River Flats is something of a hidden gem in Minneapolis's vast park network. It doesn't receive the fanfare of places like the Chain of Lakes and Minnehaha Falls, but it's a lovely entry point to the Mississippi Gorge Regional Park area that lines the river throughout Minneapolis. Up the hill from the river, Tower Hill Park is home to the highest natural point in Minneapolis and has the views to match. The famous Witch's Hat Tower that sits atop serves as an orientation point for miles around.

Start: On the east side of the University of Minnesota boathouse, just east of the parking lots for East River Flats Park

Distance: 4.3-mile round-trip

Hiking time: 1.5 to 2 hours

Difficulty: Easy; two fairly steep climbs, both on paved trail

Trail surface: Mostly blacktop; brief boardwalk along the river and some dirt trail through forest

Best season: Year-round

Other trail users: Cyclists

Canine compatibility: Leashed dogs permitted

Land status: Public city parks and public city streets

Fees and permits: Pay parking lots; annual parking permits available

Schedule: 6 a.m. to 10 p.m. daily

Trail contacts and maps: Minneapolis Park & Recreation Board; (612) 230-6400; minneapolisparks.org

Finding the trailhead: From I-94, take exit 235B for Huron Boulevard. Continue on Huron Boulevard for 0.1 mile and turn left onto Fulton Street SE, heading west. After about 0.3 mile, Fulton Street SE intersects SE Harvard Street and merges into East River Parkway. Continue heading west for another 0.3 mile. The entrance for East River Flats Park will be on your left. Take the driveway downhill into the park. The boathouse adjacent to the trailhead is near the eastern edge of the parking lot. GPS: N44°58.18667' / W93°13.91333'

The Hike

Tucked below the University of Minnesota campus, East River Flats is a gateway to the beautiful Mississippi Gorge Regional Park area. Just up the bluffs, Tower Hill Park—home to the local landmark known as Witch's Hat Tower—provides

Descend to the Mississippi on these stairs built against the bluffs. DAVID BAUR

stunning views of the Minneapolis skyline. Your 4.3-mile hike brings the two together and gives you a good workout as you make your way up and down the hillsides.

Begin at the eastern edge of East River Flats Park, just past the boathouse for the University of Minnesota, where the trail heads southeast into the woods along the shoreline of the river. The trail passes under both I-94 and Franklin Avenue, which, while not exactly picturesque, does provide a few good looks at the limestone rock face. If you've already had your fill of the Mississippi when you reach Franklin, you can shorten the route quite a bit by taking the stairway that cuts a pretty path up the hillside and through the trees to E. River Parkway above. You'll find the stairway on the southeast side of Franklin Avenue.

Around this area you might notice a few fire pits or other evidence of people hanging around that don't exactly look official. The proximity to the University of Minnesota above and its setting in the heart of the city make the river a spot for occasional nighttime revelry. Unfortunately, this can result in people leaving evidence of their visit behind. Remember: Pack it in, pack it out!

WITCH'S HAT TOWER

Tower Hill Park is not named for the tower that's on the hill in that park. If that last sentence made no sense, here's the explanation. The name instead pays homage to a military watchtower that stood on the hill until around 1870. Though the park was originally named Saint Anthony Heights Park in 1908, a petition from local residents got it changed to its current name just a year later, all of which occurred prior to the construction of Witch's Hat Tower in 1913.

A water tower until 1952, the Witch's Hat Tower opens its octagonal observation deck just once per year, during nearby Pratt Community School's annual ice cream social. As the highest natural point in Minneapolis, Tower Hill Park is a popular spot for taking in panoramic views of the city skyline. It's also the rumored inspiration behind Bob Dylan's song "All Along the Watchtower," as it was visible from his apartment in the nearby Dinkytown neighborhood, adjacent to the University of Minnesota. Given the lyrics and the title to the song, it seems possible Mr. Dylan was just as inspired by the story of the military tower that originally stood on the site.

Beyond Franklin, you rejoin the blacktop trail. Oaks and maples keep the path shady, and a number of unmarked trails lead you down to the river itself. These tiny beaches offer people walking dogs a chance to relax beside the water while their pups splash around and wear themselves out. By now you've also reached a point of interesting dichotomy in the hike. Looking back upriver you can see the Minneapolis skyline; looking downriver to the southeast creates the illusion that you're miles from civilization. The only thing that betrays that feeling is the old rail bridge above.

The upper trail along the ridge runs alongside E. River Parkway and is very popular with cyclists, joggers, skateboarders, and more, given its proximity to the university. It's a slow and steady climb up as you venture away from the river on Franklin Avenue toward Tower Hill Park, but you're rewarded with good shade and a peaceful stroll through the "urban village" of the Prospect Park neighborhood, a streetcar suburb of Minneapolis once upon a time.

As you hike up Malcolm Avenue as it bends to the right, the top of Tower Hill Park finally comes into view over the shoulder of Pratt Community School. The top of Tower Hill Park is a great place to take a rest. Back to the west you've got spectacular views of the Minneapolis skyline as well as an up-close look at the Witch's Hat. If you listen closely, you might even be able to catch the sound of the Green Line light rail down the hill in the opposite direction, another reminder of all the ways Minneapolis balances beautiful parkland with a modern city.

Miles and Directions

- **0.0** Start at the trail on the southeast side of the University of Minnesota boathouse and hike southeast into the woods.

- **0.6** The trail crosses under the bridge for Franklin Avenue. Continue hiking southeast along the river.

- **1.2** Follow the trail as it begins to switchback uphill to the trail along E. River Parkway.

- **1.3** Atop the ridge, turn left (northwest) to head back toward Franklin Avenue, about 0.6 mile away.

- **1.9** At the Franklin Avenue stoplight, turn right (east) to cross the E. River Parkway then turn left to cross to the north side of Franklin. Follow Franklin Avenue east.

- **2.2** Turn left (north) at Malcolm Avenue SE.

East River Flats to Witch's Hat

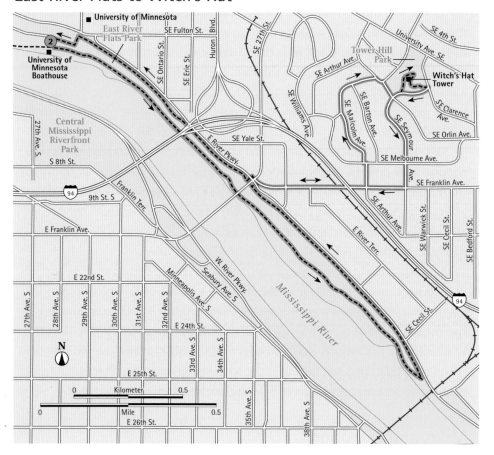

2.6 Malcolm Avenue SE intersects Orlin Avenue SE. Cross to the east side of Orlin Avenue SE and turn right (south).

2.7 Turn left (northeast) on Seymour Avenue SE. Soon thereafter, a small paved trail on your left leads uphill into Tower Hill Park.

2.8 From Tower Hill Park, descend on the trail opposite the one you came in on back to Seymour Avenue SE. At the bottom turn right (south) onto Seymour Avenue SE and follow it back down to Franklin Avenue.

3.2 Turn right (west) on Franklin Avenue to head back toward the river.

3.5 Cross 27th Avenue SE, heading west, then cross E. River Parkway to end up back on the trail on the west side of E. River Parkway.

3.6 Turn right (northwest) along the pedestrian trail on the west side of E. River Parkway to head back toward the trailhead.

4.2 Near the intersections of E. River Parkway, Fulton Street SE, and Harvard Street SE, descend the stairs back to East River Flats Park.

4.3 At the bottom of the stairs, turn right (northwest) to follow the trail back to the east side of the boathouse and arrive back at the trailhead.

Hike Information

Local Information: Meet Minneapolis; (612) 767-8000; minneapolis.org

Other Resources: Prospect Park; pperr.org

3   Chain of Lakes

The Chain of Lakes is a fantastic example of just how well interconnected the trails of urban Minneapolis truly are. Usually you'd have to flee to some remote national park, only accessible by car, to find trails that could keep you busy for 13.5 miles. That's what makes Minneapolis special. Here you can get the distance right in the city as you hike the Lake of the Isles, Lake Calhoun, and Lake Harriet.

Start: Lake Calhoun North Beach

Distance: 13.5 miles of connected loops

Hiking time: 3 to 4 hours

Difficulty: Easy terrain, difficult length

Trail surface: Paved

Best season: Year-round

Other trail users: Walkers and occasionally cyclists

Canine compatibility: Dogs permitted

Land status: Public

Fees and permits: No fees or permits required

Schedule: 24 hours a day, 7 days a week

Trail contacts and maps: Meet Minneapolis; (888) 676-6757; minneapolis.org

Finding the trailhead: Lake Calhoun North Beach is accessible from Minneapolis and Saint Paul via the Beltline Expressway and I-35. Lake Calhoun North Beach is at the intersection of Lake Street and Calhoun Parkway. GPS: N44°56.92945' / W93°18.98492'

The Hike

There's nothing difficult about this hike beyond the miles. This is an urban hike over paved pedestrian paths for the entire 13.5 miles, making it the perfect hike to catch up on old podcasts as you spend the next few hours mindlessly trekking along.

You kick things off at Lake Calhoun North Beach, which is easily reached by bus; there's a stop across the street. Traffic is a bit hairy over here, especially on Lake Street, so you really would be best served arriving without a car. However you come, start hiking east along the trail, with Lake Calhoun on your right. In under 0.5 mile, you'll already be leaving the Lake Calhoun section of the trail to take an off-ramp of sorts north to the Lake of the Isles. Hiked clockwise, this is

The walking trails around Lake of the Isles are much more calm than those at neighboring Lake Calhoun or even Cedar Lake. JOE BAUR

just a hair more than 2.5 miles. With downtown Minneapolis sitting northwest of here, you'll almost always have a great view of the skyline whenever you're hiking in that direction.

Once you finish with Lake of the Isles, you'll rejoin Lake Calhoun where you left off and continue south around the lake, surrounded by active people running, in-line skating, or paddling in the lakes. You'll continue for a little under 1 mile to reach W. 36th Street. Here you'll start the 3.3-mile loop around historic Lakewood Cemetery. So long as you're not creeped out by being in a cemetery for 3 miles, you'll find that this loop provides a great change of scenery whether you're a nerd for Minneapolis history or simply enjoy a good cemetery. Despite their purpose, historic cemeteries can be quite beautiful, and Lakewood Cemetery is no exception.

After Lakewood Cemetery, you'll come back to Lake Calhoun for another 0.5 mile of hiking before you turn off again. This time you'll be heading south for another approximately 3.0-mile loop around Lake Harriet. Finishing the Lake Harriet loop will take you to about 12 miles once you return to Lake Calhoun. From this point on, you'll follow along the western edge of Lake Calhoun until you return to North Beach. Because of the direction you're hiking, you'll enjoy some of the best views of the Minneapolis skyline as you end the hike.

CALHOUN CONTROVERSY

There's been a bit of controversy over the namesake of Lake Calhoun in recent years. For decades the name was an afterthought, with many businesses borrowing the lake's name for their own enterprises. That is until area residents realized that the lake was named for nineteenth-century US vice president and secretary of war John C. Calhoun, an avowed pro-slavery politician. Following the tragic Charleston, South Carolina, church shootings of 2015, a new push to change the lake's name has gained momentum.

Regardless of its name, Lake Calhoun will always be known as the place where guys go in the summertime for a shirtless run in hopes of impressing someone.

Miles and Directions

0.0 Start at Lake Calhoun North Beach, hiking east along Lake Calhoun.

0.3 Turn right (south) to follow the trail toward the lake. The trail quickly turns back north to go underneath the bridge you were just walking on.

0.5 Stay to the left (northwest) and follow the trail until you reach Lake of the Isles Parkway.

0.6 Cross the parkway and turn left (west) to hike clockwise around Lake of the Isles.

3.3 Return to the start of the Lake of the Isles loop. Cross Lake of the Isles Parkway; keep left (south) and follow until you return to where you turned right at 0.3 mile.

3.6 Back where you left Lake Calhoun, continue south around Lake Calhoun, with the water on your right.

4.4 Reach the junction for the loop around Lakewood Cemetery. Turn left at W. 36th Street and hike east away from Lake Calhoun. You'll hike briefly in a shared pedestrian-bike lane.

4.7 Arrive at the entrance of Lakewood Cemetery. As this is a cemetery, there are no trail names but rather pathways you can walk. For the purposes of this book, we'll stay on the outside path unless otherwise noted. To start, turn left (east) after the entrance. You'll ignore a number of pathways to stay on the outermost path.

4.9 The path starts to bend south.

Chain of Lakes

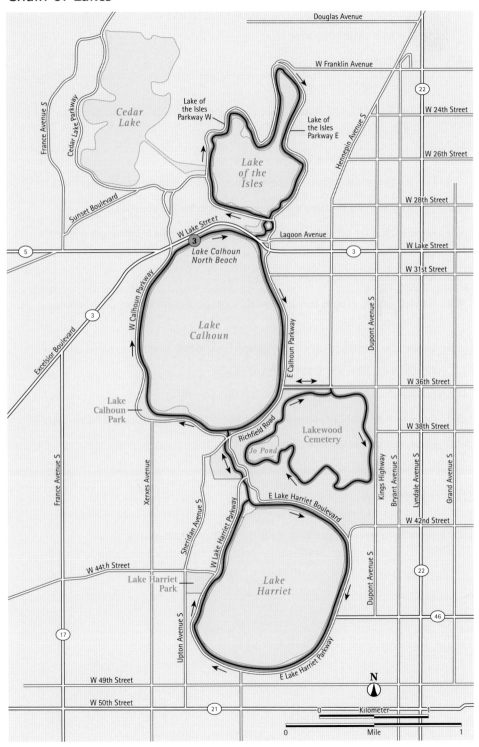

5.8 At this point you'll stop hiking on the outermost path, so don't turn left. A left turn (downhill) doesn't lead to anything exciting. Instead, continue straight, following the path as it bends southwest.

6.1 The path turns northwest.

6.2 Continue straight, hiking northwest.

6.4 Turn left (west) toward Jo Pond. Once at Jo Pond, in less than 0.1 mile, turn left (south) to hike clockwise around the body of water.

6.8 Continue straight (east) alongside Jo Pond.

6.9 Turn left (north) and remain on the outermost path toward the cemetery entrance.

7.2 The path bends right, taking you east toward the cemetery entrance.

7.4 Arrive back at the cemetery entrance and retrace your steps to where you left Lake Calhoun along W. 36th Street.

7.7 Return to Lake Calhoun and turn left (south).

8.2 Turn left (south) to cross over the bike path and head down William Berry Parkway toward Lake Harriet.

8.6 Turn left (southeast) to start hiking around Lake Harriet. Simply stay on the path for about 3 miles until you return to this junction.

11.5 Retrace your steps back to where you left Lake Calhoun.

12.0 Arrive back at Lake Calhoun and turn left (west) to finishing hiking around the lake.

13.5 Arrive back at Lake Calhoun North Beach.

Hike Information

....

Local Information: Meet Minneapolis; (612) 767-8000; minneapolis.org

4 Summit–Capitol Loop

From the Governor's Residence to the State Capitol and back, this loop takes you past some of Saint Paul's most iconic historical landmarks in a tour of gorgeous architecture and incredible views. This 5.5-mile hike proceeds down Summit Avenue through the Historic Hill Heritage Preservation District toward the Cathedral of Saint Paul en route to the Capitol building designed by famed architect Cass Gilbert, a pioneer in the building of skyscrapers. Heading back, you'll pass the home of railroad magnate James J. Hill and stop for stunning views across the river bluffs at Nathan Hale Park.

Start: Near the intersection of Lexington Parkway and Summit Avenue, on the south side of Summit

Distance: 5.5-mile lollipop

Hiking time: About 2 hours

Difficulty: Easy, with one gradual incline of about 0.8 mile

Trail surface: Sidewalk

Best season: Year-round

Other trail users: Cyclists

Canine compatibility: Licensed dogs on leashes of 6 feet or less permitted

Land status: City streets and city park

Fees and permits: No permits required; pay parking on some streets if you choose to begin at a different point

Schedule: 24 hours a day, 7 days a week

Trail contacts and maps: Visit Saint Paul; (800) 627-6101; visitsaintpaul.com

Finding the trailhead: From I-94, exit onto Lexington Parkway heading south. After approximately 0.7 mile, turn left onto Summit Avenue. Park at any available curbside parking location. GPS: N44°56.48500' / W93°08.77167'

The Hike

Recognized by the American Planning Association as one of "10 Great Streets for 2008," Summit Avenue is home to hundreds of mansions from the city's boom era during the Gilded Age and into the early twentieth century. This includes the Minnesota Governor's Residence, which is a contributing structure to the Historic Hill District that this hike traverses.

This statue in Summit Overlook Park is called "New York Eagle" and originally perched on the New York Life building in Saint Paul until its 1967 demolition. DAVID BAUR

Originally built for Saint Paul businessman Horace Hills Irvine, the Governor's Residence was donated by Irvine's daughters to the state of Minnesota in 1965. Though Summit is lined with dozens of massive homes, the Governor's Residence stands out. It seems as though it was built specifically for the purpose of housing a head of state. The residence is used by the governor today, and tours are available if you're interested, though they are somewhat infrequent. Best to plan ahead.

When Summit intersects Dale Street, it's worth continuing just a hair east of Dale to check out 599 Summit Avenue. Here stands the home of author F. Scott Fitzgerald and the first of two National Historic Landmarks featured on this route. Though the writer lived there for only a short time, it is seen as a heavy influence on his writing and was where he wrote his first novel, *This Side of Paradise*.

> Borrow or share gear among friends and family, or consider renting items you may not use often. Donating used gear to nonprofit organizations is a great way to extend its life if it's still in good, usable condition.

After you head north on Dale and then turn east onto Selby Avenue, another important Saint Paul landmark comes into view. The gorgeous Cathedral of Saint Paul stands on Cathedral Hill overlooking the Capitol and downtown. An active Catholic church, the Cathedral of Saint Paul is home to the Archdiocese of Saint Paul and Minneapolis. In addition to its official religious capacities, it is also recognized for its architectural and historic importance and is a popular tourist destination.

When you reach the cathedral, the Minnesota State Capitol building will be in sight down John Ireland Boulevard. Designed by Cass Gilbert, a forefather of skyscrapers, the Capitol is another architectural wonder, extensively renovated recently. It must be said that the stretch of road leading to the Capitol building is less appealing than the rest of the hike, as the serpentine network of on- and off-ramps built to serve I-35 E and I-94 have detracted some from the area's original elegant layout.

Back up from the Capitol past the cathedral, you rejoin Summit Avenue on its eastern terminus heading west, where you'll soon pass the home of railroad magnate James J. Hill on your left. Like the Fitzgerald house, this gem is a National Historic Landmark and another contributing structure to the Historic Hill District. It's a popular tourist attraction, and it seems a school field trip takes place there daily.

Continuing southwest, Summit approaches Ramsey Street at Nathan Hale Park. This tiny spot draws more than its share of visitors owing to its stunning views to the south. It's a great place to relax for a few minutes.

JAMES J. HILL HOUSE

Even among the other colossal houses on Summit Avenue, the James J. Hill House stands out. With more than 36,000 square feet, it was recognized as both the largest and most expensive home in the entire state when it was completed in 1891. Designed in the Richardsonian Romanesque style, the home is recognized as an important example of precisely the type of Gilded Age mansions that make Summit Avenue famous. The home's staggering size may be ostentatious, but it seems a fitting relic for a railroad tycoon like James J. Hill and the era in which he lived. His Great Northern Railway from Saint Paul to Seattle was privately funded, making it the only transcontinental railway built without government land grants, and his legacy lives on in many ways. One of those includes the use of his nickname, "The Empire Builder," for the Amtrak route that connects Saint Paul to Seattle to this day.

At this point, you could simply retrace your steps by staying on Summit Avenue. Instead, follow the sidewalk down Summit Court into one of the most-secluded neighborhoods in Saint Paul. It's lined with more beautiful homes and incredibly quiet, despite being in the middle of the city.

From here the hike heads west down Grand Avenue. You'll pass dozens of bars, shops, and restaurants. If it's hot out, stop for some ice cream at Grande Ole Creamery to give yourself something to savor for the remainder of the hike.

Miles and Directions

0.0 Start at the intersection of Lexington Parkway and Summit Avenue and hike east on Summit.

1.0 Turn left (north) at the intersection of Summit Avenue and Dale Street. (*Option:* The F. Scott Fitzgerald House, a National Historic Landmark, is less than 1 block east of the Dale Street intersection.)

1.3 Turn right (east) at the intersection of Dale Street and Selby Avenue.

1.9 Take the trail that cuts northeast through Boyd Park at the intersection of Virginia Street and Selby Avenue.

2.0 Turn right (east) onto Dayton Avenue at the northeast corner of Boyd Park.

2.3 Turn left (northeast) on John Ireland Boulevard at the intersection with Dayton Avenue toward the Minnesota State Capitol.

2.6 John Ireland Boulevard ends at Rev. Dr. Martin Luther King Boulevard, which encircles the southern end of the Minnesota Capitol, separating the upper and lower mall areas. The hike turns around in front of the Capitol building to head back uphill toward the cathedral.

2.8 Retrace your steps by following John Ireland Boulevard back to the southwest, crossing I-94 and then Kellogg Boulevard again.

3.2 Back at the Cathedral of Saint Paul, John Ireland Boulevard becomes Summit Avenue. Take Summit Avenue southwest from the cathedral.

3.9 Turn left (south) onto Summit Court just after the intersection of Summit Avenue and Ramsey Street.

4.1 At the intersection with Lawton Street, Summit Court becomes Grand Hill and bends west.

Summit–Capitol Loop

4.3 Turn left (south) onto Oakland Avenue then immediately turn right (west) onto Grand Avenue.

5.4 Turn right (north) on Lexington Parkway.

5.5 Arrive back at the beginning of the loop.

Hike Information

....

Local Information: Visit Saint Paul; (800) 627-6101; visitsaintpaul.com

Local Events and Attractions: Cathedral of Saint Paul, 239 Selby Ave., Saint Paul; (651) 228-1766; cathedralsaintpaul.org

Grand Old Days; grandave.com

James J. Hill House, 240 Summit Ave., Saint Paul; (651) 297-2555; sites.mnhs.org/historic-sites/james-j-hill-house

The Minnesota Governor's Residence, 1006 Summit Ave., Saint Paul; (651) 201-3464; mn.gov/admin/governors-residence/

Restaurants: W. A. Frost and Company, 374 Selby Ave., Saint Paul; (651) 224-5715; wafrost.com

Grand Ole Creamery & Grand Pizza, 750 Grand Ave., Saint Paul; (651) 293-1655; ice creamstpaulmn.com

The Happy Gnome, 498 Selby Ave., Saint Paul; (651) 287-2018; thehappygnome.com

Hike Tours: Summit Avenue Walking Tours; Minnesota Historical Society; (651) 297-2555; mnhs.org

Other Resources: Minnesota Historical Society; mnhs.org

5   Bunker Hills Regional Park

Welcome to the northernmost hike detailed in this book. Come for the miles of paved and unpaved trails through restored prairies and forest; stay for everything else. With a golf course, playgrounds, an archery range, and even a water park, Bunker Hills Regional Park offers so much to do that you might want to reserve a spot at the campground and stay a while.

Start: Trailhead just south of the Bunker Hills Activity Center in the southwestern corner of the parking lot of Bunker Lake Boulevard NE

Distance: 5.2-mile lollipop

Hiking time: 1.75 to 2.25 hours

Difficulty: Easy, with paved trails on gently rolling hills

Trail surface: Paved blacktop

Best season: Year-round

Other trail users: Cyclists

Canine compatibility: Leashed dogs permitted

Land status: Public regional park

Fees and permits: Anoka County vehicle permit required, either day pass or annual; annual permits also valid in Washington County and Carver County parks

Schedule: 6 a.m. to half hour after sunset

Trail contacts and maps: Anoka County Parks & Recreation; (763) 757-3920; anokacounty.us/372/Parks-Recreation

Finding the trailhead: From I-35 W, north of downtown Minneapolis, take exit 30 for US 10 W toward Anoka. Drive northwest on US 10 W for approximately 2.2 miles and take the MN 65/Central Avenue exit. Follow MN 65/Central Avenue NE for 5.8 miles. Turn left onto Bunker Lake Boulevard NE and head west for 2.1 miles. After passing Jefferson Avenue, take the next left onto CR D. The trailhead is in the southwest corner of the first parking lot, shortly after the entrance. GPS: 45°12.98333' / W93°16.62500'

The Hike

Like many other parks, Bunker Hills offers a network of both paved and natural-surface trails to choose from. The key distinction at Bunker Hills is that the paved and unpaved trails are less duplicative than some places, with each covering distinct parts of the park and creating different experiences. The unpaved paths

A bur oak stands alone in the fields on the edges of the Bunker Hills trails. DAVID BAUR

draw closer to lake itself, connect to the campground in the heart of the park, and then weave through hills on the park's southern edge. The paved trails form the most natural and easily navigable loops. For that reason, the hike described here uses the paved trails to create a lollipop. The step-by-step instructions will point out some of the best options for venturing off the beaten path.

There's plenty to like about Bunker Hills, but the star of the show has to be the boardwalk that bisects the northeastern corner of Bunker Lake. Many parks contain boardwalks, but few have the scale of the one here. Checking in at over 1,000 feet end to end, it cuts right through the marshy grasses that ring the lake. At the peak of summer, these grasses stretch to eye level, even with the boost from being on the elevated walkway.

After crossing the boardwalk and heading south on the west side of the lake, your path cuts back to the southeast through forest that includes a noteworthy presence of conifers in addition to red pines, some spruce, and maybe even a fir or two. If you want to hug the lake a little more, this stretch is a good spot to venture off the blacktop for a while.

On the southern segment of the hike, which begins near the horse stables, the paved trail flanks the tangled web of natural-surface trails with the campground in the middle. These run mostly north–south, occasionally intersecting

WHAT'S "GREEN" AND EATS CO_2?

Biochar is a charcoal product made from plant material. It occurs as a by-product of pyrolysis (decomposition caused by high temperatures), which is part of the process to create biofuels like biodiesel and synthetic gasoline. The interest in biochar is as a possible "soil amendment," something you can add to your soil to improve its suitability for growing things. In addition to its potential to improve soil quality and plant yields, biochar also absorbs and holds carbon dioxide. This means it could be a powerful tool in reducing the amount of carbon dioxide in the atmosphere.

the main path. When you rejoin the blacktop, you'll want to take a moment to get your bearings.

Bunker Hills is packed with recreational amenities, and they've got to go somewhere. Much of the western portion of the route wraps around Bunker Beach Water Park and passes alongside playgrounds and picnic areas. Though the trail is still pretty, the somewhat frequent intersections with entryways to the park can take you out of the moment.

As consolation, just after passing the parking lot for the water park, you'll hike through a long corridor of tall, beautiful conifers before emerging into an area of restored prairie and winding north. If, like your authors, you're a sucker for the sound of a train in the distance, listen closely as you head north on the hike's western edge. Just off to the west, you may hear the rumbling of the BNSF freight rail route that connects the Twin Cities to Duluth and beyond.

Near the end of your hike, after retracing your path across the boardwalk, consider exploring the biochar garden area just north of the activities center. It's part of a research project conducted by the Master Gardener program at the University of Minnesota's Anoka County extension. It's intended to determine the viability of biochar (see sidebar) for use in home gardens.

Miles and Directions

0.0 Start at the trailhead just south of the Bunker Hills Activity Center in the south-western corner of the parking lot. Hike northwest behind the activity center.

Bunker Hills Regional Park

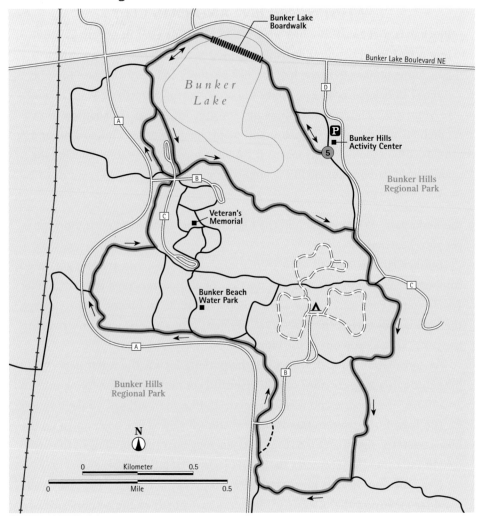

0.3 Arrive at the eastern terminus of the boardwalk across Bunker Lake. Proceed across the boardwalk, heading west and slightly north.

0.5 Turn left (southwest) soon after crossing the boardwalk.

0.6 At the split in the trail, bear left (south).

0.8 At another split in the trail, take the left branch to continue southeast.

1.0 Turn left (east) at the multi-way intersection of CR B and CR C.

1.6 The trail approaches CR D and bends right. Follow it south through the trail intersection, about 0.1 mile later.

2.1 Turn left (south) at the trail intersection. Going straight here leads to the trailhead near the campground visitor center.

2.4 Turn right (west) when the trail comes to a T at another paved trail.

2.7 Veer right as the trail approaches CR A to head north.

2.9 Continue north by crossing CR B. The trail then bends west as it traces CR A.

3.2 *Bailout:* Just before Bunker Beach Water Park, you can follow the trails north to skip the westernmost section of the route.

3.4 Continue west through the corridor of trees and continue tracing CR A just past Bunker Beach. The trail will soon bend north.

3.7 Continue north and then east when the trail splits to your left.

3.9 Turn left (north), passing between CR A and CR C.

4.1 Cross CR B to continue north. The trail soon bends east briefly.

4.4 Turn left to head north toward the boardwalk for Bunker Lake.

4.5 Turn right (northeast) toward the lake. Cross the boardwalk again, heading southeast.

5.2 Arrive back at the trailhead.

Hike Information

Local Information: Explore Minnesota; (888) 847-4866; exploreminnesota.com

Other Resources: Anoka County Master Gardeners; anokamastergardeners.org/projects/biochar_garden

International Biochar Initiative; biochar-international.org/biochar

6 Elm Creek Park Reserve

As the largest park in the Three Rivers Park District, with more than 50 miles of trails available to hikers, Elm Creek Park Reserve is a place you can visit again and again without doing the same route twice. Stop in at Eastman Nature Center to check out the exhibits and wildlife observation deck before venturing out to hike the loops that ring the nature center.

Start: Trailhead on the west side of Eastman Nature Center

Distance: 5.6-mile loop

Hiking time: About 2 hours

Difficulty: Easy, with wide trails and only mild inclines

Trail surface: Forest floor, grass, and blacktop

Best season: Year-round, though especially great for fall colors

Other trail users: Cyclists on paved segments

Canine compatibility: Dogs permitted with a 6-foot, non-retractable leash on paved trails

Land status: Public park within the Three Rivers Park District

Fees and permits: No fees or permits required

Schedule: 5 a.m. to 10 p.m. daily

Trail contacts and maps: Three Rivers Park District; (763) 694-7860; threerivers parks.org

Finding the trailhead: From I-94, take exit 213 for Maple Grove Parkway toward CR 30. Turn right onto Maple Grove Parkway and head northeast for 1.3 miles. Turn right onto CR 81, heading southeast. Take the very next left to turn north onto Fernbrook Lane. After 1.1 miles turn right onto Elm Creek Road. In about 0.6 mile turn right at the sign for Eastman Nature Center; follow the road to the parking lot. GPS: 45°09.29167' / W93°27.00500'

The Hike

Eastman Nature Center serves as the hub of Elm Creek Park Reserve's network of hiking trails, so that's where you'll begin. Before that, take a few minutes to explore the nature center. Its 14,000 square feet contain classrooms and reading rooms, professional exhibits where you can watch wildlife, and an open-air deck. With so many activities offered, the place is abuzz, particularly on weekends.

Grab a coffee and a copy of the trail map for the area surrounding Eastman for your hike before hitting the trails.

Find the trailhead on the west side of the nature center and head south into the floodplain forest. In addition to the six hiking loops that orbit the nature center are more than 17 miles of bridle trails and extensive paved paths. The intersections are all well marked, but you'll probably need to double-check a few times before deciding which turn you want to take. The hike outlined here touches at least part of all of them, and you can make a perfectly satisfying trip on just these trails.

Begin heading south on the western edge of the Heron Trail on your way to the Oxbow Loop, which crisscrosses Rush Creek several times on sturdy wood bridges. As natural surface paths, they are susceptible to becoming a bit slick if there's a stretch of rainy weather, but the park clearly makes an effort to keep them dry. Some of the obvious washouts have large gravel stones to help facilitate drainage, and park personnel put down sandy dirt to help in other spots as well.

The Oxbow Loop soon rejoins the Heron Trail, and not long after that you pick up the Monarch Trail, heading east. If it's a busy day at Elm Creek, you'll start to feel the crowds thin a bit the farther you get from the nature center. By

The trails around Eastman Nature Center crisscross Rush Creek. HOLLY BAUR

the time you're on the Creek Trail, there's a good chance you'll feel like you have the place to yourself.

When the trail turns south on the eastern edge of the route, you emerge from the shade of the hardwoods, and the trail becomes sunny and grassy for a while. This area is a popular hangout for garter snakes, though you probably won't see them until they're slithering away as you go by. Whether this is an exciting brush with nature or deeply terrifying will depend on how you generally feel about snakes. If the prospect of sharing your hike with snakes is a turnoff, keep in mind that garter snakes pose no danger to humans, and you can always stick to the blacktop trails, which they seem to avoid.

The Pierre Bottineau house serves as an exhibit of Minnesota's frontier past, of which Bottineau is an important figure. As a surveyor, he helped found numerous cities, including Osseo and Maple Grove, where Elm Creek Park Reserve is located. Today his name lives on in the form of Bottineau Boulevard in Hennepin County, as well as Bottineau Park and Bottineau Library in northeast Minneapolis.

When the Creek Trail and its extensions come to an end, you can either take up the blacktop as you head west or find the bridle trail. If you choose blacktop, at the southernmost portion of the route you will see a sign indicating that the Medicine Lake Trail is accessible to the south. You can follow that path briefly to check out the historic house of Pierre Bottineau, a famous Minnesota frontiersman. It was built in 1854 as the first home in what is now Maple Grove Township, though the building's current location is at least its fourth.

Heading back north on the park's west side, the trail hugs Fernbrook Lane. When the driveway for Rush Creek Campground intersects your path, turn right and head toward the campground. From there you can pick up the southwestern edge of the Meadowlark Trail to make your way back toward the nature center. Have a seat on the bench along the way to enjoy the view over the prairie, rewarding yourself for a hike well done.

Miles and Directions

0.0   Start at the trailhead on the west side of Eastman Nature Center and hike south, following signs for the Heron Trail and Oxbow Loop.

Elm Creek Park Reserve

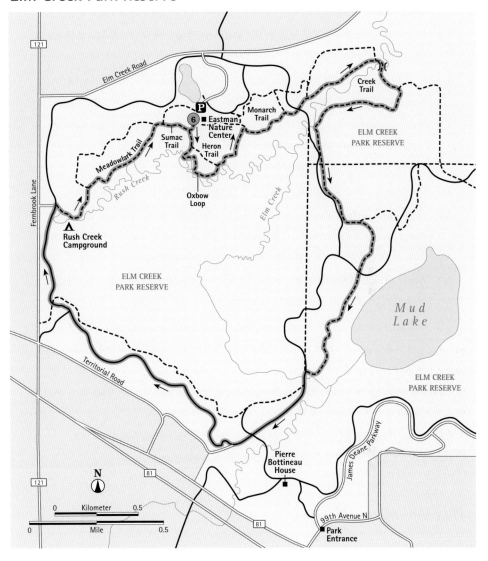

0.1 The trail splits, with the southern edge of the Heron Trail heading to your left (east). Continue south through this intersection, heading toward Rush Creek and beginning the Oxbow Loop, where you'll cross several bridges.

0.3 The Oxbow Loop ends at this intersection with the Heron Trail. Turn right to head northeast, crossing the final bridge.

0.5 The Heron and Monarch Trails connect. Turn right to follow the southern edge of the Monarch Trail to the east.

0.7 The path splits to your left at the eastern edge of the Monarch Trail. Begin the Creek Trail by continuing northeast for 0.5 mile, crossing the blacktop path on your way.

1.2 Cross the bridge over Elm Creek as the path begins to turn south. Follow it through the woods and then uphill as it turns back west.

1.5 A trail branches off to your right; continue straight, heading east. (*Option:* A small loop branches from the main trail for about 0.2 mile before rejoining the trail.)

1.9 The trail approaches a multi-way intersection; remain on the path heading south. (*Bailout:* Turn right to join the blacktop train and head north. This will lead back toward the trails for Eastman Nature Center.)

2.5 Continue heading slightly southwest, as the path intersects the paved trail.

3.0 The natural surface trail comes to a T at the blacktop trail. Turn left to take the paved trail to the southwest. (*Option:* A horse trail heading west from this location follows almost the same path as the blacktop but is more rustic.)

3.3 Proceed through this intersection as the trail reaches its southern tip. (*Side trip:* Turn right to visit the Pierre Bottineau house.)

4.8 Just after crossing Rush Creek, turn right to follow the driveway east toward Rush Creek Campground. Pick up the trail on the north side of the campground, heading uphill to the northeast.

5.1 The trail connects with the southwestern edge of the Meadowlark Trail. Turn right to continue northeast along Meadowlark's southern segment.

5.5 Reach the southwestern corner of the Sumac Trail; turn right (east).

5.6 Arrive back at the trailhead.

Hike Information

Local Information: Explore Minnesota; (888) 847-4866; exploreminnesota.com

Other Resources: Minnesota Historical Society; legacy.mnhs.org/projects/2211

7 Crow-Hassan Park Reserve

A number of hikes in this book contain sections of oak savanna, but it's tough to beat the one at Crow-Hassan Park Reserve in the northwest metro area. With over 17 miles of rustic trails open to hikers and wide-open vistas, it's a great place to spot bald eagles soaring overhead. Don't be fooled—the prairie's deceptive flatness masks rolling hills made more challenging by sandy trails. You might get more of a workout than you expect.

Start: Trailhead on the north side of the grass-and-dirt parking lot on Park Preserve Road

Distance: 4.6-mile loop

Hiking time: About 1.5 hours

Difficulty: Moderate, with extremely soft, sandy trails and rolling hills

Trail surface: Natural surfaces, including forest floor, dirt, and grass; several horse trails with rutted tracks and a sandy base

Best season: Year-round

Other trail users: Equestrians on marked trails

Canine compatibility: Dogs permitted with a 6-foot, non-retractable leash on marked trails

Land status: Public park within the Three Rivers Park District

Fees and permits: No fees or permits required

Schedule: 5 a.m. to 10 p.m. daily

Trail contacts and maps: Three Rivers Park District; (763) 694-7860; threerivers parks.org

Finding the trailhead: From I-94 W, take exit 207A-207B for MN 101 toward Rogers/CR 81 and continue about 0.6 mile. Use the second lane from the left to turn onto MN 101, heading south. Choose the middle lane to stay on MN 101 S as it becomes Main Street. Main Street briefly becomes Industrial Boulevard. Make a slight right to take Main Street, heading south for 1.1 miles. Turn right onto Territorial Road and head northwest for 2.3 miles. Turn left onto Hassan Parkway, heading southwest for 1.6 miles. At the intersection with Park Drive, turn right to head north and then almost immediately turn left onto Park Reserve Road. Head west for 0.5 mile to the parking lot. GPS: 45°11.10500' / W93°37.76833'

The Hike

There's no doubt that most parks in the Minneapolis–Saint Paul area do a fantastic job of being accessible to people of all ages, interests, and fitness levels. Most have a wide range of recreational amenities available and networks of paved trails that make it easy to get around, as well as unpaved ones for a true hiking experience. But sometimes it's nice to get truly away from all that, and you can at Crow-Hassan Park Reserve. You'll find nothing but rustic, unpaved trails as you hike through beautiful restored oak savannas.

A significant chunk of the route outlined here includes bridle trails, and even on sections that are not technically for horses, it's clear they sometimes get used that way. Bridle trails are common in many of the hikes in this book, but horseback riding is noticeably more popular at Crow-Hassan than at many other spots. There are, frankly, piles of evidence on the trails to support this assumption, so watch your step.

Begin your hike at the trailhead on the north side of the parking lot and head north. After a short jaunt through forest, you'll arrive at your first intersection, marked #10. Like some other parks, Crow-Hassan is easily navigated by using its numerical intersection markers. The step-by-step directions below will call out

Prairie grasses catch a breeze just up from South Twin Lake. DAVID BAUR

Blue asters line the trails through the prairie in summer. DAVID BAUR

each number specifically, and if you carry a map, GPS unit, or smartphone with you, it should be pretty easy to ensure you're on the right path.

The path heading west–southwest from marker #10 turns into the prairie, and bluestems sway in the breeze. It's a wide, grassy path where eager grasshoppers pop up around you. Soon you'll cross the service road and head uphill through the trees. The service road is open to hikers, should your desired route require it. It's worth noting that Crow-Hassan's service road is a significantly better hiking experience than most. It blends in better with the trail network than in other places where the service road is more like a true road.

When you meet up with the bridle trail on the southwest portion of the loop, near several birdhouses, the terrain gets more challenging. Horses are big and heavy, and they tend to turn the already sandy path into soft mush. The trail is not incredibly difficult, but when it's softer, it can be more taxing.

Soon your path starts swinging back north as you approach the Crow River. While in the floodplain forest, you should see a flight of rough stairs leading down to the riverbank. Watch your step heading down, but it's a worthwhile diversion. You'll continue north, passing the appropriately named Blue Stem Campground, and reenter a beautiful patch of forest as the trail becomes easier going again.

Just after you turn east around marker #7, the forest comes to an abrupt end, and you enter an epic, breathtaking expanse of restored prairie. The scale of it makes it seem as though you've come much farther than you really have, a rewarding feeling to be sure. Here the trail becomes the soft, sugary sand from earlier, making you earn these last couple miles. In late summer, pretty purple-blue asters line the way. When the path turns south again, passing between North and South Twin Lakes, you're in the homestretch. Back at marker #10, continue south to wrap up your Crow-Hassan loop.

Miles and Directions

0.0 Start at the trailhead on the north side of the grass-and-dirt parking lot on Park Preserve Road and hike north for 0.1 mile.

0.1 At the trail intersection marked #10, turn left onto the grass trail, heading west and then southwest. It will be marked for hikers only.

0.6 The trail intersects the service road that bisects the park. Continue through this intersection, heading south as you reenter the woods. Soon you emerge from the forest and head southwest.

1.1 Now at trail marker #15, take the path leading to your right to continue more directly west along the edge of the forest, tracing the Crow River.

1.6 At the three-way junction at marker #13, stay to your left and continue heading northwest along the river. (*Bailout:* Turning right here will lead you out to the service road, which you can follow back to the trailhead, about 1 mile to your east.)

1.7 Shortly after marker #13, a set of stairs on your left leads down to the river.

1.9 Veer to your right to stay on the trail. Going straight ahead here leads into the picnic and camping area of Blue Stem Campground. Feel free to stop off for a break.

2.0 At marker #9, just down the hill from the campground, follow the trail as it heads north into the woods.

2.6 The trail bends east and then reaches marker #7, where a quaint pond sits off to your south. Continue heading east here. (*Side trip:* Turning left [northeast] at marker #7 can add a loop along the northern edge of the park. You'll stay in forest longer before emerging near the Crow River and heading east, where you'll have a few options for getting back to the trailhead.)

3.3 Reach an intersection like an old country road at marker #6. Continue straight ahead (east) in the direction of North and South Twin Lakes. (*Option:* Turning right

Crow-Hassan Park Reserve

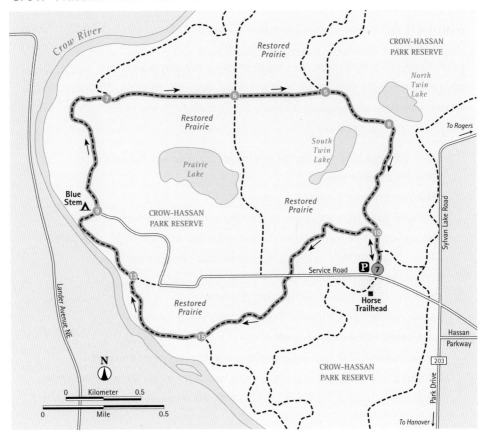

at marker #6 will take you south past Prairie Lake and then intersect the service road, which you can take east back to the trailhead.)

3.6 At marker #5, remain on your current trail, heading east to pass between the lakes.

4.0 Just to the south of North Twin Lake, turn right to head south and slightly west at marker #8.

4.5 Back at marker #10, continue straight ahead (south).

4.6 Arrive back at the trailhead.

Hike Information

Local Information: Explore Minnesota; (888) 847-4866; exploreminnesota.com

8 Tamarack Nature Center

A fun place to hike and a great place to learn about nature, Tamarack Nature Center in White Bear Township is a 320-acre preserve within the larger Bald Eagle–Otter Lakes Regional Park. Explore the trails across wetlands, prairie, and forest. If you have children with you, or are just a big kid yourself, head to Discovery Hollow Nature Play Area and Garden, a nature play area where you're not only permitted but encouraged to get dirty.

Start: Trailhead leading from the parking lot for Tamarack Nature Center

Distance: 2.9-mile loop

Hiking time: About 1 hour

Difficulty: Easy, with occasional minor hills, particularly on the south side

Trail surface: Some blacktop; mostly a combination of wood chips, grass path, forest floor, and dirt, including some areas that can get muddy

Best season: Year-round

Other trail users: Cross-country skiers in winter

Canine compatibility: Dogs not permitted on trails at Tamarack

Land status: Ramsey County park

Fees and permits: No fees or permits required, but donations accepted

Schedule: Half hour before sunrise to half hour after sunset daily. Nature center hours: Mon through Fri 8 a.m. to 4:30 p.m., Sat 9 a.m. to 5 p.m., Sun noon to 5 p.m.

Trail contacts and maps: Tamarack Nature Center; (651) 407-5350; parks.co.ramsey .mn.us/tamarack/Pages/tamarack.aspx

Finding the trailhead: Take I-35 E, heading north from downtown Saint Paul for about 9.3 miles, and take exit 117 toward CR 96. Turn right (east) onto CR 96. After 0.1 mile, turn left onto White Bear Parkway and head north and east as the road bends for 1.3 miles. At Otter Lake Road turn left; continue north for 0.8 mile and turn left into the entrance for Tamarack Nature Center. GPS: N45°06.09667' / W93°02.21500'

The Hike

Right up against an interstate might not be the first location most folks would think of for a great park, but Tamarack Nature Center makes lemonade out of those lemons. You'll begin your hike at the trail that points right at the actual

Tamarack Nature Center's southeastern section gets quite marshy, and some trails may not be passable as a result. DAVID BAUR

nature center building, but almost immediately you'll branch into the forest at the sign that conveniently notes "Trail Access Here." It's like they knew what you were looking for! The park also has named trails, something many other parks lack, and includes numbered intersections to make your navigation even easier.

After that brief patch of woods, you'll turn into open prairie and head west, where you'll soon pass little Teal Pond. This section is known as the Goldenrod Trail. It's got a pretty view to your south and west, and your right side to the north is lined with conifers that include pine, spruce, and, of course, the pretty tamarack trees for which the park is named.

There's really no way to avoid this. When your trail reaches the western edge of the park, you're all but certain to hear highway

> Tamarack trees, the conifers for which this park is named, are also known as larch trees.

noise unless it's the middle of the night, at which point the park is closed and you probably shouldn't be there. The good news is that it's not oppressively loud, and the reason the trail is called Goldenrod becomes more evident.

Soon the wood-chip Tamarack Trail branches off to your left and takes you closer to Tamarack Lake, if that's the route you choose. The Goldenrod Trail also continues cutting southeast, parallel to the Tamarack Trail, but our route

FLOATING TREATMENT WETLANDS

Eutrophication caused by high phosphorous levels is a common problem in Minnesota's lakes, leading to algal blooms that pollute water sources. There are success stories, but it remains a challenging problem. The phosphorous levels at Tamarack Lake were found to exceed the state's acceptable levels, leading to its placement on the state's Impaired Waters List. To combat this problem, a floating treatment wetland was installed to help filter pollutants from the water. These "wetlands" are built from recyclable materials, such as soda and water bottles, and injected with foam so that they'll float and support growth above. Floating treatment wetlands are covered with plants that make them look like small, pretty islands that might exist naturally, but they're simultaneously working hard to create microbial health below.

branches off to the south toward Fish Lake for a worthwhile extension to your hike. The official park maps mark this section as the most challenging segment of trail at the park—and it is—but it is pretty brief and not difficult enough to be intimidating.

The dirt path of the Fish Lake Trail is wide and well maintained as it passes near the southern border of the park. When it heads uphill into the woods to the south of the lake for which the trail is named, look for grouse and deer foraging nearby.

You can follow the Fish Lake Trail almost all the way to the eastern edge of the park, a patch of wetlands to the south, but be advised that the area where the trail rejoins the Goldenrod Trail and heads north typically floods over in summer. You can take your chances of course, but if you prefer, just head back northwest at marker #11 and merge with the Tamarack Trail. At marker #6 take the short trek out to the dock, where you can see the Tamarack Lake's floating treatment wetland, which is part of a project to improve water quality (see sidebar). **Note:** In warm weather, wasps like to hang out on the boardwalk leading to the dock.

After leaving the dock, your hike retraces its path briefly before heading toward the trailhead. If you're there during nature center hours, be sure to pop in and learn a bit more about the area, or at least stop off in the adjacent Discovery Hollow and Garden. You, or at least any children with you, might get to build a tree fort or make a dam. How cool is that?

Miles and Directions

0.0 Start at the paved trail heading west toward the nature center. Take the wood-chip trail heading northwest into the woods. Shortly after entering the woods, stay to your right when the trail splits to continue northwest.

0.1 The trail begins to emerge from forest and comes to a split. Stay to your right to continue northwest on the Goldenrod Trail into the grassland area. You soon pass Teal Pond on your left.

Tamarack Nature Center

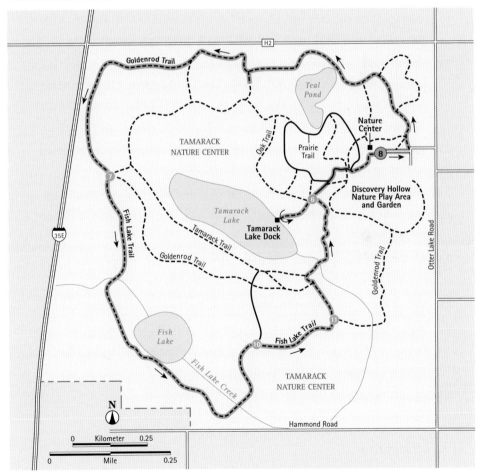

0.4 Arrive at another split, the first of two in short succession. Continue heading west through both of them. (*Option:* Turning left at either intersection will lead you to the Tamarack Trail, which runs closer to Tamarack Lake.)

0.8 The trail bends to your left and turns south along the highway.

1.0 At this three-way intersection, marked #7, take the right-hand turn to continue heading southeast on the Fish Lake Trail. Stay on this trail for the next 1 mile. (*Options:* A left turn leads to the Tamarack Trail; continuing straight ahead remains on the Goldenrod Trail.)

1.7 At the southern tip of the route, the trail bends to your left, heading northeast out of the woods and back into the prairie.

1.8 At trail marker #10, turn right to continue east toward the wetlands on the final segment of the Fish Lake Trail. (*Bailout:* Turn left at marker #10 to head north on the section called Meadowlark Trail, and trim off the eastern segment of the hike.)

2.0 Now at marker #11, turn left to head northwest in the direction of Tamarack Lake, rejoining the Goldenrod Trail. (*FYI:* You can turn right at marker #11, which heads toward Discovery Hollow and Garden, but this section of the Goldenrod Trail floods seasonally and may be impassable.)

2.2 Look for a small set of stairs on your right. Descend these steps, heading northeast to meet up with the Tamarack Trail.

2.4 At trail marker #6, turn left and follow the signs that lead toward the dock on the boardwalk to your southwest. (*Note:* Signs warn that wasps are known to land on the boardwalk.)

2.5 The floating treatment wetland is visible from the dock, and an informational sign tells you more. When you're ready, retrace your steps to marker #6.

2.6 Back at marker #6, continue straight ahead on the blacktop trail heading northeast.

2.8 The blacktop trail arrives at the Tamarack Nature Center building. You're encouraged to visit, or you can turn right to finish your hike. The Discovery Hollow and Garden is also nearby, on your right to the south.

2.9 Arrive back at the trailhead.

Hike Information

Local Information: Explore Minnesota; (888) 847-4866; exploreminnesota.com

9 Lake Rebecca Park Reserve

Combining Big Woods (a hardwood forest), forest, marsh, and wetland with lovely Lake Rebecca itself, there's something for everyone at Lake Rebecca Park Reserve. Though the park is particularly stunning dressed in fall colors, its paved trails make it easy to visit year-round. It's also part of the Three Rivers Park District's restoration program for trumpeter swans, helping bring the birds, which are considered threatened in Minnesota, back to strength and giving you a good shot at seeing them in action.

Start: Where the paved trail meets the main parking lot for Lake Rebecca

Distance: 6.5-mile loop

Hiking time: 2 to 2.5 hours

Difficulty: Moderate, due to length and a few long, steady climbs

Trail surface: Blacktop

Best season: Good year-round destination, with fall colors a particular draw

Other trail users: Cyclists

Canine compatibility: Dogs permitted with a 6-foot, non-retractable leash on paved trails

Land status: Public park within the Three Rivers Park District

Fees and permits: No fees or permits required

Schedule: 5 a.m. to 10 p.m. daily

Trail contacts and maps: Three Rivers Park District; (763) 694-7860; threerivers parks.org

Finding the trailhead: Take I-394 west until it becomes US 12 west of I-494. Drive west on US 12 for approximately 16.6 miles. Turn right onto County Line Road SE. After about 1.5 miles, County Line Road SE veers slightly right and becomes Rebecca Park Road, which you take north for another 1.2 miles. Turn right onto 66th Avenue N at the entrance for Lake Rebecca Park Reserve. The parking lot nearest the trailhead is on your right-hand side after about 0.2 mile, just past the driveway toward the boat launch. GPS: N45°04.30500' / W93°45.15833'

The Hike

Though unpaved trails are often preferred for hiking, practical considerations can make paved routes a good choice. Using the bridle trail at Lake Rebecca for hiking, which is perfectly acceptable and encouraged, makes for quite a long hike

Efforts to restore water quality have paid great dividends at Lake Rebecca. DAVID BAUR

with some noteworthy climbs. By all means, go for it! The 6.5-mile paved loop around Lake Rebecca Park Reserve is no slouch and has a few solid climbs of its own. It also runs along the southern shore of Lake Rebecca, whereas the horse trail swings far afield from the lake. For these reasons, the blacktop seemed like the better route for most folks and is what's outlined below. Although official park maps imply that the 3.7-mile mountain biking loop is not open to hikers, signage at the park says differently. It's good to have options, right?

Choosing the paved route, the hike starts unremarkably as it passes behind the parking lots heading northeast. Not to worry; it improves greatly as you leave the parking area behind and pass a park map where the trail bends to the southeast. You'll slice along a ridge through a beautiful bit of forest, with maples and basswoods arching above you and light sneaking through where it can. Segments like this make the place a popular fall color destination.

> If you're toting food, leave the packaging at home. Repack your provisions in ziplock bags that you can reuse and that can double as garbage bags on your way out of the woods.

Barely more than 1 mile in, you'll cross East Lake Rebecca Road, a gravel-and-dirt rural route that bisects the park from north to south. Look both ways before crossing of course, but traffic is pretty much nonexistent. A little while later

BETTER LIVING THROUGH CHEMISTRY

Better living through chemistry? Maybe, in the case of Lake Rebecca. Not long ago, this lake had such massive algal blooms, and the corresponding decay, that its fish were dying. Invasive species like the (sadly) nearly ubiquitous Eurasian milfoil were also a problem, a result of too much phosphorus arriving as runoff from nearby farms and homes in a process called eutrophication.

A nearby horse farm, in particular, was identified as part of the problem and became part of the solution as well. The farm's owners took measures to prevent runoff from manure—a big help, but not enough on its own. Using money from Minnesota's Clean Water, Land, and Legacy Amendment to the state constitution, which commits the state to protecting both natural resources and its arts and cultural heritage, the Three Rivers Park District began using herbicides and other chemicals to kill invasive species. Today, fish populations are growing, and the park no longer has to cordon off the swimming area in summer due to algal blooms.

the path approaches a small picnic area with a memorial for a man called Don Myron. It's the first ideal place to connect with the unpaved horse trail if you wish, though if you pick it up here heading south, it's also the stretch that takes you away from the lake.

When the trail bends back to the west, you approach the southern portion of the lake. The tree cover grows sparse for a bit, the path lined with sumac instead of maples, before you pop back into forest and cross East Lake Rebecca Road for the second and final time. The path remains wooded west of the road, but glimpses of Lake Rebecca come into view on your right, and pleasant views over the lake open up when you reach its southwestern edge.

The trail here intersects the mountain-biking route, offering a bailout heading north back to the trailhead. It's also around this point that the paved trail turns south and uphill. It's not a particularly steep climb, but it's persistent for maybe 0.5 mile or so as you head toward the southern border of the park near Kasma Marsh. You'll intersect the mountain bike trail again, cross a dusty service road, and draw hip to hip with the horse trail, all in close succession.

Swinging north around Kasma Marsh, be on the lookout for trumpeter swans, identified by their distinct black bills and all-white plumage. They are the

The treetops create a tunnel along Lake Rebecca's paved trail. DAVID BAUR

Lake Rebecca Park Reserve

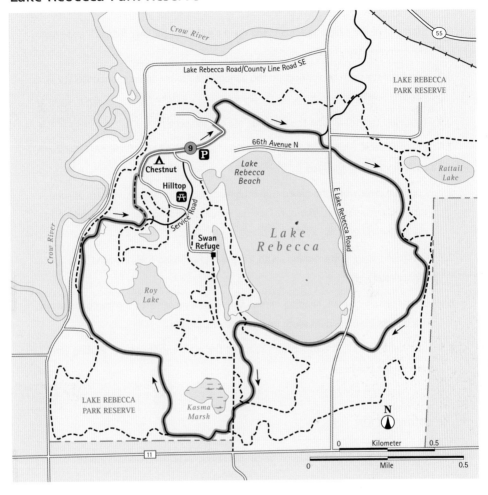

largest species of waterfowl in North America and are quite impressive to see in action when they unfurl their wings, which can span as much as 10 feet.

What goes up must come down. Enjoy the gradual descent as the path splits between two small ponds along the western front. But what goes down sometimes must come back up again. The hike takes on one last substantial climb heading east, with Lake Rebecca's smaller sibling, Roy Lake, off to your right. When you pass through the pretty Hilltop Picnic Area, you'll know the trailhead is close.

Miles and Directions

0.0 Start where the paved trail meets the main parking lot for Lake Rebecca and cross the entrance road, heading north.

0.2 Cross the service road connecting the parking area to the maintenance facility, heading northeast.

0.9 Turn right (south) around the east side of Lake Rebecca.

2.6 Continue west when the trail again intersects E. Lake Rebecca Road near the south-eastern corner of the lake.

3.2 Continue west when the paved trail intersects the mountain-biking path. It soon turns south and uphill. (*Bailout:* Take the mountain-biking trail north to return to the trailhead along the western side of Lake Rebecca.)

3.7 Continue through intersections with the mountain-biking trail a second time and a service road.

6.1 Cross the service road, heading north. (*Side trip:* A refuge area for trumpeter swans is a bit less than 0.5 mile south down the service road.)

6.5 Turn right (east) as the trail comes to a T at the main entrance road, leading you back to the trailhead.

Hike Information

Local Information: Explore Minnesota; (888) 847-4866; exploreminnesota.com

Other Resources: Minnesota's Legacy; legacy.leg.mn

Star Tribune; startribune.com/hennepin-county-s-lake-rebecca-has-made-a-remarkable-comeback/208251171/

10 Wolsfeld Woods Scientific and Natural Area

Hiking the Wolsfeld Woods Scientific and Natural Area is like learning a really great secret, the kind you'll have no problem keeping all to yourself. Hidden behind a nondescript trailhead in the northeast corner of the Trinity Lutheran Church parking lot, easily missed unless you know it's there, is a 3.1-mile hike through a fantastic Big Woods forest of the sort that was once common in the region. It's an excellent place for birders, with more than 150 species recorded, including 12 duck and 27 warbler species.

Start: Trailhead in the northeast corner of the parking lot for Trinity Lutheran Church

Distance: 3.1-mile double-loop lollipop

Hiking time: About 1 hour

Difficulty: Moderate due to mostly unmaintained, forest floor surface trails and a couple of brief climbs

Trail surface: Forest floor

Best season: Open year-round but recommended in spring for wildflowers and autumn for colors

Other trail users: Cross-country skiers and snowshoers in winter; mountain bikers and equestrians on designated trails

Canine compatibility: Dogs not permitted at Wolsfeld Woods

Land status: Minnesota Department of Natural Resources Scientific and Natural Area

Fees and permits: No fees or permits required

Schedule: 8 a.m. to 10 p.m. daily

Trail contacts and maps: Minnesota Department of Natural Resources—Scientific and Natural Area Program, Central Region; (651) 259-5800; dnr.state.mn.us/snas/index.html

Finding the trailhead: From I-394 W, continue as I-394 becomes US 12 W. Stay on US 12 W for 4.3 miles and take the exit toward Long Lake/Orono/CR 112. Continue onto what becomes Wayzata Boulevard for 1.9 miles. Turn right onto N. Brown Road. After about 0.7 mile, N. Brown Road intersects 6th Avenue N/CR 6, with Trinity Lutheran Church directly across 6th Avenue. Cross 6th Avenue N to enter the church parking lot; the trailhead is in the northeast corner of the lot. GPS: N44°59.97833' / W93°34.44333'

The Hike

Wolsfeld Woods is a state Scientific and Natural Area, meaning it's not so much a park as a scientific and educational preserve (see sidebar for more on this designation). Amenities are at a bare minimum here—for example, trails exist but are not actively maintained, and there are no restrooms. This makes for a fun hike that's deeply immersed in nature, but you'll want to come prepared. Hiking boots are even more advisable than usual, as the thick tree cover can keep the underlying trails damp, and you'll be crossing a creek a few times where, depending on recent rain levels and the route you choose, it's possible you'll have to step right into the water.

Keep your map, GPS unit, or smartphone handy, or consider snapping a picture of the map at the interpretive sign. The trails are marked to let you know whether they are for horseback riding or just hiking, but they tend to turn back on themselves, and trail junctions do not have the comprehensive "you are here" maps common in other parks. Orient yourself based on Wolsfeld Lake to the north and the creek slicing from the northwest to the southeast of the area, and you'll be fine.

Though these warnings make it seem as though the trails at Wolsfeld Woods are rugged and uneven, they're mostly easy to navigate and smooth going—a forest floor bed made softer by the leaves of seasons past. Begin by hiking a couple hundred feet up a small hill through low branches to emerge under a canopy of gorgeous hardwood trees including maple, basswood, and more. The trailhead's unremarkable beginnings make it feel a little bit like stepping through a portal to another world.

The eastern trails of Wolsfeld Woods take you past an area of emergent marsh and on a ridge above the creek that connects to Wolsfeld Lake to the northwest. Once at the creek crossing, you may find a makeshift bridge of downed trees and branches covering the gap. If you've got the right gear and aren't sure about the bridge's construction quality, it might be easier to step right into the water.

Across the creek, the trail approaches the houses that bump up against Wolsfeld Woods. Pay no mind to the tennis court that seems to appear from nowhere. It's the backyard of a nearby resident, so no need to pack your racket. Heading back northwest toward the lake, pay close attention to your map and where you turn, as this is the area where the trail network seems most confusing.

The trails are narrow but fun under a thick tree canopy at Wolsfeld Woods. DAVID BAUR

SCIENTIFIC AND NATURAL AREAS PROGRAM

Minnesota's Scientific and Natural Areas (SNAs) program was created by the 1969 Minnesota Legislature, and its mission is to "preserve and perpetuate the ecological diversity of Minnesota's natural heritage, including landforms, fossil remains, plant and animal communities, rare and endangered species, or other biotic features and geological formations, for scientific study and public edification as components of a healthy environment."

This mission means that Wolsfeld Woods and the other 160 or so SNAs around the state present not only unique opportunities for visitors but special responsibilities as well. SNAs are open to the public and can bring you closer to undisturbed nature, rare plants and animals, and unique natural landforms than more recreation-oriented parks. But as a visitor you accept an obligation not to engage in activities that might disturb the area's natural conditions, which includes things we often think of as harmless. For more information, contact the Minnesota Department of Natural Resources or visit the SNA website at dnr.state.mn.us/snas/index.html.

The lake sneaks up as surprisingly as the tennis court, though it's much prettier and less out of place. It's a good spot to look for some of the more than 150 bird species that have been seen at Wolsfeld Woods, including the red-shouldered hawks that nest in the area. (*Option:* If you head right, you can follow the trails to the north and tack on an extra loop that passes near the Wolsfeld Homesite, where the German homesteaders who gave the place its name lived.) However, the hike featured here turns left around the lake's southern tip before heading northwest. You'll cross the creek again right where it meets the lake and then turn right to walk along its southwestern edge. Just after that crossing, you can bail out by turning left and heading back. Otherwise, turn right and cross the creek yet again to tackle the steepest climb of the hike.

A half mile later, you'll reach your turnaround point, where you'll begin making your way downhill. If you've wandered out of the woods and into a clearing, you've gone too far. The 0.5 mile return completes the loop when you arrive back at the junction near the creek where the earlier bailout point was mentioned. One last, smaller climb awaits; then head back downhill again, where the trail comes to a T. A right turn puts you on the path back to the trailhead to complete your Wolsfeld Woods visit.

Miles and Directions

0.0 Start at the northeastern corner of the parking lot for Trinity Lutheran Church, where the trailhead is marked. Hike northeast into the forest.

0.2 Stay to your right to hike east as a trail enters on your left.

0.3 Turn right (south) at the four-way intersection.

0.4 Turn left (east) along the ridge above the creek when the trail comes to a T.

0.6 The trail along the ridge bends to the northeast as it descends toward the creek. Cross wherever it is easiest to do so, and rejoin the trail on the opposite side continuing northeast.

0.7 Continue northeast when another trail enters on your left.

Wolsfeld Woods Scientific and Natural Area

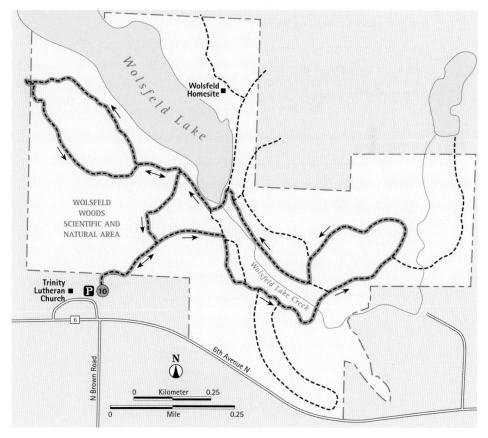

0.9 Veer left (northeast) where the trail signed for hikers only splits from the one signed for horses and hikers. You will soon bend back to the west and uphill. (*Note:* This area of trails may be somewhat difficult to navigate. In general, you should head west and south back toward the creek until the 1.2-mile mark outlined below.)

1.1 The trail splits, with the path to your right heading northwest. Continue to your left, bearing south.

1.2 Turn right (northwest) to follow the ridge above the creek toward the lake.

1.5 Turn left (southwest) at the southern end of Wolsfeld Lake, emerging from the forest. After turning, stay to your right to hug the shoreline, heading northwest.

1.7 At another intersection in the trail, continue on the trail to your right and climb the hill, heading northwest.

1.9 Take the right (northwest) path at the split in the trail at the top of the hill.

2.2 This is the turnaround point for the northwestern loop. Turn left (south).

2.6 Arrive back at the intersection from 1.9 miles. Turn right (east) to head downhill.

2.7 Turn right (south) to head up the hill.

2.9 Turn right (southwest) when the trail comes to a T at the intersection from the 0.2 mark at the beginning of the hike.

3.1 Arrive back at the trailhead.

Hike Information

Local Information: Explore Minnesota; (888) 847-4866; exploreminnesota.com

Other Resources: Friends of Wolsfeld Woods; wolsfeldwoods.org

Scientific & Natural Areas Program; (651) 259-5088; dnr.state.mn.us/snas/index.html

11 Minnesota Landscape Arboretum

With a history stretching back more than a hundred years to its 1908 origin as the Horticultural Research Center, the Minnesota Landscape Arboretum is a special place and an enormously popular destination in the Minneapolis–Saint Paul metro area. Its extensive gardens of trees, wildflowers, grasses, shrubbery, and more serve as living monuments to Minnesota's varied wetland, prairie, and forest ecology. As part of the University of Minnesota's College of Food, Agricultural and Natural Resource Sciences, the arboretum is as noteworthy for its research and education efforts as it is for its enviable beauty.

Start: Branch of the Wood Duck Trail, heading southwest from behind the Maple Syrup House

Distance: 4.0-mile lollipop

Hiking time: About 1.5 hours

Difficulty: Moderate; some climbs on rustic trails with uneven footing, particularly on the eastern half of the route

Trail surface: Blacktop, wood chips, forest floor, grass, and dirt

Best season: Spring through autumn, but worth visiting any time of year

Other trail users: None

Canine compatibility: Dogs not permitted, other than service dogs and during occasional "All About Dogs" days

Land status: Public arboretum and garden

Fees and permits: Free admission for children 12 and under; entrance fee for visitors age 13 and older. Entrance is free to paid annual members, and the arboretum offers "Free Thursdays" all day Nov through Mar and after 4:30 p.m. Apr through Oct.

Schedule: Open 363 days a year (closed on Thanksgiving and Christmas Day). Apr through Sept, the grounds are open 8 a.m. to 8 p.m.; 8 a.m. to sunset other times of the year. The many facilities and buildings within the arboretum operate on a variety of different schedules. Please check the website for specific details.

Trail contacts and maps: Minnesota Landscape Arboretum; (952) 443-1400; arboretum.umn.edu

Finding the trailhead: From I-494 near Eden Prairie, take exit 11C toward US 212 W. Merge onto US 212 and head west for 1.2 miles. Take the MN 5 W/ Arboretum Boulevard exit and continue west on MN 5 W/West 78th Street/ Arboretum Boulevard for approximately 7.5 miles. About 0.6 mile after crossing

Hazeltine Boulevard, turn left onto Arboretum Drive. GPS: N44°51.77500' / W93°37.00000'

The Hike

You really can't go wrong at the Minnesota Landscape Arboretum. If there's any problem with the place, it's that, as the largest public garden in the Upper Midwest, there's so much to see and do, it'll probably take you several visits to see everything. But that's just an excuse to keep coming back—and probably a good reason to become a member as well. This 4.0-mile hike serves as an introduction to the arboretum, ensuring that you see at least a bit of everything, but it's certainly not exhaustive. With so much variety, it can seem as though something new comes into bloom each week. That said, if you're only going to make one trip to the arboretum, it's tough to beat the fall colors.

With over 300,000 visitors annually, the arboretum is often busy, something you should definitely anticipate on weekends and on free days in particular. The crowds get thickest around the central hub formed by the Oswald Visitor Center and the Leon Snyder Building, so beginning your hike by picking up the Wood Duck Trail at the Maple Syrup House is a good way to jump right into the

Early twilight casts the Minnesota Landscape Arboretum in beautiful light and shadow with Green Heron Pond peeking through in the distance. HOLLY BAUR

FRUIT, GLORIOUS FRUIT

The Minnesota Landscape Arboretum began life as the Horticultural Research Center in 1908. The history of fruit breeding at the University of Minnesota actually goes all the way back to 1878, and the Horticultural Research Center was an outgrowth of the importance of fruit farming and breeding to the state. Since the 1920s, the University of Minnesota has introduced more than one hundred different fruit cultivars, carefully researching and breeding them for a variety of genetic properties including color, their ability to survive in cold climates, and, of course, flavor. The breeding process is meticulous and difficult, with only 1 to 2 percent of seedlings proceeding beyond the initial phase of testing.

Varieties of blueberries, raspberries, cherries, and strawberries are among the many fruits produced, but apples are the university's biggest claim to fame. For years it produced minor regional hits like Haralsons, but they hit the big time with the delicious Honeycrisp, which entered the market in 1991 and has become popular around the world. The Honeycrisp cultivar has been so successful that in 2006 the Minnesota Legislature gave it official standing as the State Fruit of Minnesota.

experience while dodging the throngs. The trail is adjacent to the main parking lots, just northwest of the visitor center. If you have to park even farther out to the northwest, you can jump on the trail's northwestern trailhead instead.

Walk west on the wood-chip Wood Duck Trail. (Now say that five times, fast.) It's a gentle path encircling Wood Duck Pond and a good spot to see deer. If you hear a rapid drumbeat coming from the forest, it might be a pileated woodpecker hard at work. You probably won't want to take the whole Wood Duck loop, as it'll lead you back into the parking area, but it's such a nice segment that it's worth going at least a little past your eventual turn uphill to the Bennet-Johnson Prairie. You'll pass briefly through the prairie section, filled with bluestem, goldenrod, and asters as you head farther south.

After crossing Three Mile Drive, which cuts a scenic meander through the arboretum, you'll pick up the paved walkway and pass through the Prairie Garden and into a series of tree collections. You'll pass through sections of birch, crabapple, and maple. Off to your south you'll pass a quirky sculpture garden on your way through the Shrub Walk and into the circular Shrub Rose Garden. The route outlined here turns back north at this point, heading down the hill from

Listen for pileated woodpeckers hard at work along the gentle Wood Duck Trail. HOLLY BAUR

the rose garden toward the Green Heron Trail and onto the trails out to the east side of the arboretum's grounds. If you're still in the mood for more tree collections, continue south to see pines, tamaracks, lindens, oaks, and more.

The bottom of the hill from the rose garden can be a bit confusing. You'll need to cross Three Mile Drive again, but this time the point where you pick up the trail is much less clear. Walk in the grass for a brief spell; the dirt trail leading northeast to Green Heron Pond soon enters on your right. For a place that has such an extensive and well-maintained network of trails, it's an odd omission not to have a clear connector here.

Follow the trail east as it swings around the edges of Green Heron Pond. Head along the pond's edge on a boardwalk, and stop off at the pier to look back west. It's a particularly pleasant view at twilight. From here you'll turn around and head east into the eastern network of trails, where numbered intersections help with navigation. You'll make a loop along Spring Peeper Trail before turning around to come back along Ridge Trail. It's a fun and occasionally strenuous 1.5 miles or so through hills and wetlands before you wind up back at the center of the arboretum near the Snyder Building.

Minnesota Landscape Arboretum

Miles and Directions

0.0 Start at the branch of the Wood Duck Trail heading southwest from behind the Maple Syrup House.

0.3 Continue past the first split in the trail to keep ringing clockwise around Wood Duck Pond. (*Option:* Turn left [southwest] if you don't want to retrace your steps to head uphill to the prairie at this junction.)

0.7 Retrace your steps back to the intersection at milepoint 0.3 when the edge of the Wood Duck Trail nears the parking lots.

1.0 Turn right (southwest) to head uphill to Bennett-Johnson Prairie.

1.2 Turn left (southeast) to head a little farther uphill. Then turn right (southwest) and follow the path as it heads downhill toward Three Mile Drive.

1.4 Cross Three Mile Drive to enter the Prairie Garden area. Pick up the paved trail on the east side of the garden area leading toward the woods.

1.5 Veer right as the trail enters the woods area.

1.8 Cross Three Mile Drive twice more as you continue heading east.

2.0 Turn left (north) just before the Shrub Rose Garden to head downhill.

2.2 Cross Three Mile Road. For maybe 100 feet or so, there is no formal trail, only a patch of grass. Hike northwest on the grass and then turn right (northeast) when the dirt trail appears.

2.3 Turn right (southeast) at the intersection onto the Green Heron Trail.

2.5 At marker #7 stay to your left to remain on the Green Heron Trail.

2.6 Turn right (east) at trail marker #3 onto the Spring Peeper Trail.

2.7 At marker #4 continue east on the Spring Peeper Trail.

3.0 Turn left (north) onto the Ridge Trail at marker #5.

3.6 Turn right (west) at trail marker #2, still on the Ridge Trail.

3.8 Turn right (northwest) at marker #1 to head uphill to the visitor center.

3.9 Continue northwest behind the Snyder Building and then cross between that building and the adjacent Oswald Visitor Center.

4.0 Arrive back at the trailhead.

Hike Information

Local Information: Explore Minnesota; (888) 847-4866; exploreminnesota.com

Other Resources: History of Fruit Research; arboretum.umn.edu/fruitbreeding.aspx

Minnesota State Fruit; mn.gov/portal/about-minnesota/state-symbols/fruit.jsp

12 Minnesota Valley National Wildlife Refuge—Louisville Swamp

Lining the Minnesota River for almost 70 miles, the Minnesota Valley National Wildlife Refuge contains multiple areas to visit. But the roughly 7-mile hike around the Louisville Swamp Unit offers something special. Here you'll find some of the best floodplain forests and wetlands around, filled with mature trees and wildlife. On top of that, you get views of the river valley and an up-close look at a massive boulder from Minnesota's glaciated past. By the time you're done, any negative connotations the word *swamp* might conjure will be wiped away.

Start: Trailhead for the Mazomani Trail on the south side of the main parking lot for the Louisville Swamp Unit of the Minnesota Valley National Wildlife Refuge

Distance: 7.2-mile loop

Hiking time: About 2.5 hours

Difficulty: Strenuous due to length and challenging trails, which are unpaved, lightly maintained, and potentially wet and muddy

Trail surface: Grass, forest floor, and dirt that is often muddy; brief stretch of crushed red gravel

Best season: Spring after snow thaw through late autumn; trails not maintained in winter and can be covered in packed ice

Other trail users: State Access Trail sections open to equestrians, cyclists, and snowmobilers; all other sections for hikers only

Canine compatibility: Leashed dogs permitted on trails where indicated

Land status: National wildlife refuge

Fees and permits: No fees or permits required

Schedule: Sunrise to sunset daily

Trail contacts and maps: Minnesota Valley National Wildlife Refuge; (952) 854-5900; fws.gov/refuge/Minnesota_Valley/

Finding the trailhead: Follow US 169 south from where it meets I-494 for approximately 15.8 miles. Turn right onto 145th Street, heading west. The parking lot is on your left after about 0.4 mile. GPS: N44°44.40000' / W93°35.84167'

The Hike

It's okay to admit it if the word *swamp* doesn't make you think of somewhere you'd like to hike, but it's also hard to imagine your regretting it if you give Louisville Swamp the shot it deserves. Speaking of shots, several parts of the Minnesota Valley National Wildlife Refuge, including Louisville Swamp, are open to spring and fall seasonal hunting, so you might want to check your dates before heading over.

Begin your hike in the dusty parking lot where the State Trail Access Trail and the Mazomani Trail come together, and take a look at the entrance sign before heading in to double-check for trail closures due to water levels. It's a marsh area, after all. In particular, there is a small segment of the Mazomani Trail called Flood's Road that, given its name, stands a good chance of being closed on your visit. This hike assumes you'll skip that. You'll want to pack your insect repellent, too, but that's a good practice in general.

You begin in oak savanna on a grassy trail winding down a ridge on your way to the wetlands below. Heading to the south after the split in the Mazomani Trail takes you to the level of the marsh and your first real taste of swampy trail. As you enter the forest, maples grow in clusters arching overhead, intermixed with

One of the many ponds at Louisville Swamp is wreathed in yellow flowers. DAVID BAUR

No sign of the swamp to come at the start of the trail, but trust me, it's there. DAVID BAUR

box elder and cottonwood. Underfoot, in addition to the mud, you'll occasionally come across a surface of large stones embedded in the ground—the leavings of the glaciers that covered the region not that long ago in geologic terms. Tread carefully on these, as they can be quite slick when damp.

A pattern soon emerges in your hike, which you may notice around the time you cross the bridge over Sand Creek

The Minnesota Renaissance Festival is Louisville Swamp's neighbor to the north, and you'll likely see signs for it as you approach. Open weekends from late August through early October, it draws over 300,000 visitors annually, making it the largest Renaissance festival in the United States.

around the 1.0-mile mark. In segments that are more of the open wetland variety, the trail can be quite narrow as grasses and other plants grow right up to the edges. Entering the forest, where the undergrowth is sparse, brings breathing room.

Reaching the southeastern corner of your hike, the Mazomani Trail emerges rather suddenly from the woods into open wetlands, where you'll make a hard right onto Middle Road to head west. It's worth deviating from the route briefly to visit the giant glacial boulder that marks the junction. Returning to Middle Road, it's not long before the Mazomani Trail branches off from the crushed red rock and gravel of Middle Road to the northwest. That's where you'd head to complete the Mazomani loop if Flood's Road is open, but this hike continues west.

The hike along Middle Road is probably the least exciting segment of the hike, but its openness lets you watch for birds soaring above and provides a reprieve from mosquitoes. From Middle Road you head into the Carver Rapids area, where you can deviate to the north to visit the Jab's Farm historical site and see ruins of the old farmstead. Otherwise, continue toward Johnson Slough en route to the State Corridor Trail that traces the Minnesota River, passing a couple of small ponds ringed in yellow wildflowers in summer.

Northbound on the State Corridor Trail, you'll pass through another segment of forest, where leopard and chorus frogs may flee from your footfalls. The solitude of the forest can make it easy to forget, but you're now hiking alongside the Minnesota River. You'll get some nice reminders of its presence and views to match the farther north you go.

Just before turning back south, you'll cross Sand Creek a second time and head up a steep, challenging hill. It's mercifully short at least, and your reward

> Consider citronella as an effective natural mosquito repellent.

is to hike along a ridge heading south, where you can occasionally steal glances out over the valley to the northeast. Your hike comes to an end along the State Trail Access Trail, heading east along a peaceful field. It's a welcome way to wrap up your visit.

Miles and Directions

0.0 Start at the trailhead for the Mazomani Trail, in the main parking lot for the Louisville Swamp, and hike south.

0.2 Beginning at this marker, you'll pass a couple of unmarked trail intersections. Stay left to head toward the southbound route clockwise around Louisville Swamp.

0.5 Come to the signed intersection for the Mazomani Trail. Stay to your left to head south.

1.1 Cross the bridge over Sand Creek to continue south.

1.6 Cross a second bridge, still continuing south.

2.2 The Mazomani Trail emerges from the forest at the intersection with Middle Road. Turn right to head west on Middle Road.

2.3 Shortly after turning onto Middle Road, the Mazomani Trail branches off to your right, heading northwest. Though your route continues on Middle Road, you may wish to view the giant glacial boulder that marks this split. (*Option:* If Flood's Road along the Mazomani Trail is open, you can complete the full Mazomani loop by taking this trail northwest.)

2.8 Middle Road comes to an intersection. Turn right to head north along the southern portion of Flood's Road.

3.0 Arrive at a Y split in Flood's Road. Take the left trail to head west. (*Option:* If you choose to head north here, you can visit the Jab's Farm historic ruins and also complete a small loop on the Johnson Slough Trail.)

3.5 The southern portion of Flood's Road intersects the State Corridor Trail. Turn right here to head north near the Minnesota River.

3.9 Pass Johnson Slough on your right. Continue following the trail north for the next 1.6 miles as it traces the river.

Minnesota Valley National Wildlife Refuge—Louisville Swamp

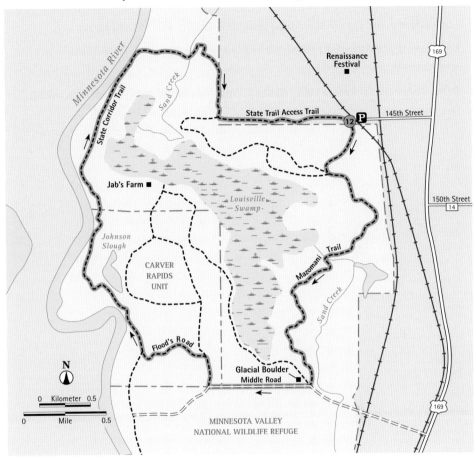

5.5 The trail bends to your right, turning east and away from the river.

5.8 Cross Sand Creek for the second time and head sharply uphill, still going east.

5.9 After cresting the hill, turn right at the intersection with the State Trail Access Trail to head south along the ridgeline.

6.4 Turn left to head straight (east), following the State Trail Access Trail for the next 0.8 mile.

7.2 Arrive at the eastern trailhead of the State Trail Access Trail, which exits into the parking lot.

Hike Information

....

Local Information: Explore Minnesota; (888) 847-4866; exploreminnesota.com

Local Events and Attractions: Minnesota Renaissance Festival; (952) 445-7361; renaissancefest.com

Other Resources: Minnesota Valley National Wildlife Refuge Hunting Regulations & Map; fws.gov/uploadedFiles/For%20Webite%202012%20Brochure%20Option.pdf

13 Cleary Lake Regional Park

Cleary Lake Regional Park might have the happiest visitors in the Twin Cities. You'll be greeted with smiling faces and waves from walkers and cyclists alike on the route around Cleary Lake before ducking into the nearby woods and prairie to get off the beaten path for the second half of the hike. Look for ospreys in their nesting area near the lake, and watch your step as leopard and chorus frogs fill the grassy forest trails. It's an easy, relaxing walk through this popular south metro park.

Start: On the east side of Park Road, where the blacktop trail intersects the road next to the visitor center

Distance: 5.1-mile loop

Hiking time: 1.5 to 2 hours

Difficulty: Easy, with wide, flat trails

Trail surface: Blacktop for the first half; a mix of grass and forest floor for the second

Best season: Year-round

Other trail users: Cyclists

Canine compatibility: Dogs permitted with a 6-foot, non-retractable leash on paved trails

Land status: Public park within the Three Rivers Park District

Fees and permits: No fees or permits required

Schedule: 5 a.m. to 10 p.m. daily

Trail contacts and maps: Three Rivers Park District; (763) 694-7860; threerivers parks.org

Finding the trailhead: Head south for 12.3 miles on I-35 W from where it meets I-494, passing the junction with I-35 E on your way. Get off at exit 84 for 185th Street W toward Dakota CR 60. Turn right onto 185th Street, heading west for 2.2 miles, at which point it becomes Eagle Creek Avenue. Travel northwest on Eagle Creek Avenue for about 2.3 miles to the intersection with Texas Avenue. Turn left to head south on Texas Avenue for about 0.6 mile and then turn right onto Park Road to enter Clearly Lake Regional Park. The parking lot for the park is on your right in about 0.5 mile. GPS: N44°41.34833' / W93°23.27833'

The Hike

Hiking at Cleary Lake is pretty much the definition of taking a stroll. In contrast to the steep hills at nearby Murphy-Hanrehan Park Reserve, the trails here are wide, flat, and smooth. Start your hike on the blacktop trail just north of the visitor center and on the western edge of Cleary Lake Golf Course. You'll spend about half your trip hiking the paved loop around the lake before heading into the woods and prairie on the unpaved trails in the park's southwest section.

Making your way counterclockwise around the lake, you'll have to get out of the parking lot area first. Calls of "fore!" and the *thwack* of hitting a golf ball greet your ears just to the east, while the sound of children comes at you from the beach to the west. Not to worry. After just 0.3 mile or so, the path breaks away from the action around the park's many amenities. When you reach the northeastern corner of the hike, where it approaches Eagle Creek Avenue, there is an opportunity to take an unpaved trail northwest. It'll take you farther from the lake and will add some distance if you want a longer hike, but it's also much closer to the noise of the road than the blacktop route.

The path around the lake is lined with sumac that turns a beautiful, rich red in fall, bright goldenrod, and pretty purple thistle as well. Cyclists wave and smile. People paddle canoes leisurely on the lake. You'll cross a small creek that bends

Cleary Lake is a great spot for a peaceful paddle. DAVID BAUR

lazily into the lake from the north, and frequent rest areas offer a chance to relax for a bit or maybe enjoy a picnic. It's altogether idyllic and pleasant.

Heading down the west side of the lake, your suspension of disbelief might be disrupted briefly as the thinner tree cover opens up a view of nearby homes, and you might hear some cars going by. Things improve again shortly when you pass another of Three River Parks District's osprey nests, which are part of an ongoing restoration program.

> At Cleary Lake's golf course you can play footgolf, a new and growing sport that combines soccer (football) with golf. Participants kick a soccer ball, attempting to make it into a hole in as few kicks as possible, just like golf shots.

When the trail swings south and deviates from the lake, around 2.9 miles in, it intersects the unpaved trails of the park's southwestern loops at marker #9. The farthest reaches of this area are only available to skiers in winter, and be advised that flooding can close other portions. Assuming everything's a go, head into the forest on what's called the Lakeside Trail. It's something of a misnomer, as the trail leads away from the lake, not beside it.

The Lakeside Trail is a mixture of grass and forest floor but remains wide and flat. On sunny days, when you pass through the occasional stretches uncovered by tree canopy, you might find dozens of chorus and leopard frogs bouncing along. It's nigh impossible to spot them until they move, but if you want to get a good view, they sometimes stay put along the side of the trail if you come to a pause.

As you make your way back from the southwestern loops, you'll cross the service road and pass near several of Cleary's campgrounds. You'll also pass the Poplar Trail, which can add another mile or so if you're up for it. Otherwise, you'll soon meet up with the blacktop trail once more to finish alongside the visitor center.

Miles and Directions

0.0   Start at the east side of Park Road, where the blacktop trail intersects the road next to the visitor center. Hike north and stay on the trail as it bends northeast around the golf course.

Cleary Lake Regional Park

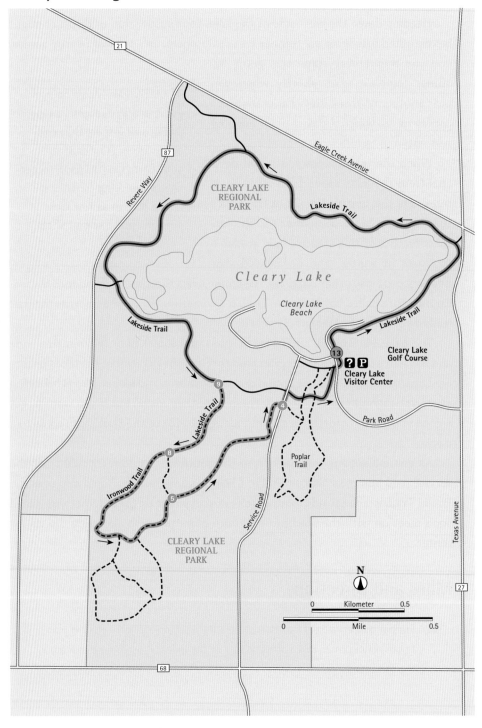

0.6 The blacktop trail splits to your right. Continue left (northwest) on the main trail. (*Option:* If you take the split to your right, you can join the unpaved trail that heads northwest, much closer to Eagle Creek Avenue.)

1.1 Cross a small creek over a bridge.

1.5 Stay to your left when the trail splits to your right. You will head a little farther west, and then the trail turns southwest.

2.0 Cross another small creek. There is a nice rest area to view the beach off to your left.

2.3 A small trail that leads out of the park enters on your right. Stay on the main path, heading southeast. You will be near the osprey nesting site at this point.

2.9 The paved trail intersects marker #9. Turn right to take the grassy Lakeside Trail, heading southwest.

3.3 At trail marker #8, continue your southwest trajectory by going straight and beginning the Ironwood Trail. (*Bailout:* Turn left at marker #8 to stay on the Lakeside Trail and shorten the loop heading to marker #5.)

3.7 Turn left at the marked bypass through the forest, heading east. The bypass does not appear on official maps but has park signage. The cut-through is very brief and will place you on the east side of the Ironwood Trail. (*Note:* This turn may depend on the season and trail conditions. The cut-through is required if the trail ahead is closed due to water levels. Otherwise, you may be able to continue on the Ironwood Trail.)

3.9 A path enters on your right that leads southeast and out into prairie. Stay to your left to remain on the Ironwood Trail. (*Side trip:* Heading southeast into the prairie is a pretty diversion that eventually leads out to the service road. You can either take it all the way to the service road and then take that road back north or make it a short out-and-back.)

4.0 At trail marker #5, continue to your right (northeast) as you rejoin the Lakeside Trail.

4.5 The Lakeside Trail exits the woods and approaches the service road. Don't cross the road. Instead, stay on the grass along the road's west side. This is the actual trail. You're only alongside the road briefly before it turns back into the woods.

4.7 Emerging from the woods again, this time cross the service road heading east toward trail marker #4. On the east side of the service road, turn left to head north along the road very briefly until you intersect the blacktop trail. Turn right (east) on the blacktop trail. (*Option:* Continue into the woods at marker #4 toward Red Pine Campground to add the Poplar Trail loop.)

4.8 The blacktop trail intersects the Poplar Trail twice in quick succession. Continue east on the blacktop trail and follow it as it passes through the woods and approaches Park Road.

5.0 Cross Park Road on the blacktop trail, heading east toward the visitor center.

5.1 Arrive back at the trailhead.

Hike Information

Local Information: Explore Minnesota; (888) 847–4866; exploreminnesota.com

14 Murphy-Hanrehan Park Reserve

Hiking the trails in the northeastern corner of Murphy-Hanrehan Park Reserve is like riding a roller coaster, or as close as you're likely to get while hiking anyway. Over the 5.8-mile hike, you'll climb rugged hills and then do your best not pitch forward and roll right down their descents. It's a fun and often challenging hike through forest and along ridges carved by glaciers many millennia ago. As an added bonus, the reserve carries the National Audubon Society's Important Bird Area designation.

Start: Trailhead behind the restroom, on the south side of the parking area located just after turning onto Murphy Lake Boulevard

Distance: 5.8-mile double loop

Hiking time: 1.5 to 2 hours

Difficulty: Strenuous, with rugged, rustic trails and several steep climbs and descents

Trail surface: Dirt, grass, and forest floor

Best season: Year-round, although about half this hike is closed Apr 1 to Aug 1.

Other trail users: None

Canine compatibility: Dogs not permitted on the trails used in this hike; leashed dogs are allowed on 3.6 miles of trails to the southeast.

Land status: Public park within the Three Rivers Park District

Fees and permits: No fees or permits required

Schedule: 5 a.m. to 10 p.m. daily

Trail contacts and maps: Three Rivers Park District; (763) 694-7777; threerivers parks.org

Finding the trailhead: Head south for 7.9 miles on I-35 W from where it meets I-494. Use the right lane to take exit 1 for CR 42 toward Crystal Lake Road. Turn right onto CR 42 W/Egan Drive, heading west for 1.9 miles. Turn left onto W. Burnsville Parkway, heading south for 1.2 miles; stay on it as it becomes Hanrehan Lake Boulevard for another 1.2 miles. At the traffic circle, take the second exit to head south on Murphy Lake Boulevard. Turn left into the parking lot after just a few hundred feet. GPS: N44°43.44667' / W93°20.87500'

The Hike

Murphy-Hanrehan Park Reserve is tucked within the edges of Twin Cities suburbia, with cul-de-sac neighborhoods on its north and east and flat, unpaved rural

One of the rare flat segments of the trails at Murphy-Hanrehan Park Reserve DAVID BAUR

roads to its south and west. The park itself stands apart, looking like none of its surroundings with its rugged, tree-covered hills. If you've got a walking stick, this is a good hike to bring it along.

Like several other Twin Cities parks, Murphy-Hanrehan uses numbered trail intersections. These make it easy to navigate—and easy to change your route on the fly if you need to. **Note:** The route described here is sort of like bringing two loops together. The eastern loop, beginning around marker #18, is closed from April 1 to August 1, so take that into consideration when planning your visit.

The hike begins on a wide, grassy path, and it's relatively easygoing to start. The biggest challenge comes from deep ruts left by the vehicles that service the trails. It's not long before you hit the first hills and enter the forest to begin heading generally uphill, albeit with frequent dips. In stark contrast to almost every other hike in this book, there's really no part of this hike that is completely flat for any meaningful length of time, but that's part of the fun.

Murphy-Hanrehan Park Reserve is also home to popular mountain-biking trails. Its challenging hiking trails are just as popular with cross-country skiers in winter.

When you reach trail marker #18 after about 1.5 miles in, you begin the seasonally available eastern part of the route. Though you've already dealt with some ups and downs on the trail, the hills get noticeably steeper on this half. Beginning at about the 1.6-mile mark, you'll make a steady climb for 0.2 mile before an extremely steep climb, where you'll gain around 100 feet of elevation in around 0.1 mile. Get a good forward lean going, and blast through it.

As challenging as grades of nearly 20 percent are to climb, descending them might be even harder. Some of the sharp descents at Murphy-Hanrehan occur on stretches of trail that are a bit gravelly, which makes them potentially slippery as well. Sometimes it's easier to almost run downhill; as noted earlier, if you've got a walking stick, it'll come in handy here.

On the eastern side of the park, you remain under a canopy of a greatest hits of Minnesota's hardwood deciduous trees. It's a decent time to consider some other good, general backwoods advice: The familiar "leaves of three, let them be," applies here. Western poison ivy is common in Minnesota's forests and is not easily distinguished from box elder saplings. Wearing long pants is not a bad idea, even on hot days.

Winding back west and south, you'll come downhill long enough to get a neat view of marsh grasses around the 4.0-mile point looking west. It's a decent spot to catch your breath, because you've got about 0.5 mile of your last major uphill from there. During that stretch you'll pass a sign that warns of a steep descent, a rather comical place for the first such warning given what's come before. Maybe more signs just weren't in the budget.

By now you're back in the western half of the loop, taking its northern half, which swings closer to Hanrehan Lake. When you cross the boardwalk through the marsh, look back to your right. It's the reverse of the vista you had at 4 miles. After the 5-mile mark, you'll get a much easier trail for some welcome relief on your return to the trailhead.

Miles and Directions

0.0   Start at the trailhead located just south of the restroom facility for the dirt parking lot off Murphy Lake Boulevard and hike south.

0.8   At this intersection, a service road called Henn Parks Road enters on your right. Turn left to follow the road for about 0.2 mile, heading east.

1.0   Turn left to veer off Henn Parks Road at marker #11, heading northeast.

Murphy-Hanrehan Park Reserve

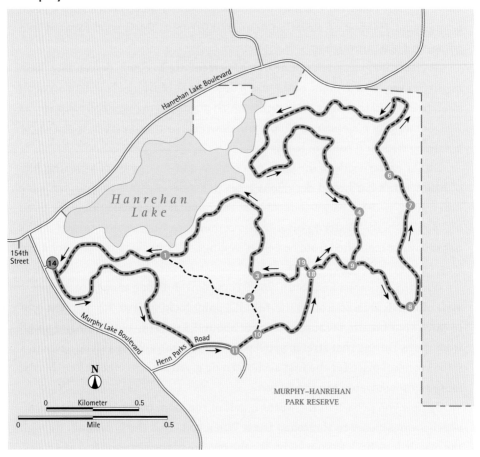

1.1 At marker #10, the trail splits to your left. Continue straight, still moving northeast. It'll soon turn more northward, heading toward marker #18.

1.4 Arriving at marker #18, turn right to head east toward marker #9. (*Bailout:* Turn left at marker #18 to head toward marker #19 and pick up the directions beginning at 4.5 miles.)

1.6 Come to marker #9. Continue straight ahead (east) to begin the eastern loop of the hike, moving counterclockwise. The next segment includes the steepest part of the hike. (*Option:* Turn left here to do the same loop in the opposite direction.)

1.8 Now at marker #8, turn left to begin heading north. The trail to your right is not open in summer.

2.2 At marker #7 you can choose either the right or left path. Either option leads to marker #6, just 0.1 mile to the north.

2.3 Marker #6 completes the small bubble in the trail. Continue heading north. The trail that heads off to your right (east) is not a designated trail.

2.6 The trail reaches its northeastern turnaround point, and you'll begin heading back west. There are no trail intersections until the 4.0-mile mark, so stick to the current path.

4.0 At marker #4 the trail splits to your right. This is another trail that's not open in summer. Continue south toward marker #9.

4.2 Back at marker #9, turn right to head west toward marker #18.

4.4 At marker #18 turn right (north) and head uphill. This connects you with the northern segment of the western loop.

4.5 Turn left here at marker #19 to head west.

4.7 Now at marker #3, turn right (north) toward Hanrehan Lake.

4.8 Cross a small boardwalk in the wetlands, heading north. The trail then bends to your left, going southwest along the outline of Hanrehan Lake.

5.3 Reach marker #1; stay to the right, which is more or less just continuing straight.

5.8 Arrive back at the trailhead.

Hike Information

....

Local Information: Explore Minnesota; (888) 847-4866; exploreminnesota.com

15 Lebanon Hills East

Lebanon Hills Regional Park is one of the most beloved parks in the Twin Cities metro area, and it doesn't take long to figure out why. It contains some of the region's most popular mountain-biking paths and a chain of lakes that's perfect for canoeing. The extensive trail network offers 19 miles of hiking on 2,000 acres across gorgeous rolling hills. This 4.1-mile hike introduces you to the eastern side of the Lebanon Hills, drawing near five of the park's many lakes and ponds through peaceful woodlands.

Start: Trailhead behind the visitor center's west side

Distance: 4.1-mile loop

Hiking time: 1.25 to 1.5 hours

Difficulty: Moderate, with rolling hills

Trail surface: Natural surfaces including grass and forest floor; very brief section of paved trail at the trailhead

Best season: Year-round

Other trail users: None on designated hiking trails

Canine compatibility: Leashed dogs permitted

Land status: Dakota County public regional park

Fees and permits: No fees or permits required

Schedule: Visitor center trailhead open 8 a.m. to 10 p.m.; other trailheads open at 5 a.m.

Trail contacts and maps: Lebanon Hills Visitor Center; (651) 554-6530; www.co .dakota.mn.us/parks/parksTrails/LebanonHills/Pages/default.aspx

Finding the trailhead: Heading south on I-35 E, take exit 98, about 0.8 mile after I-35 E meets I-494, for Dakota CR 26/Lone Oak Road. Turn left onto Lone Oak Road, heading east for around 0.4 mile. Turn right onto Lexington Avenue S. After 4.1 miles, turn left onto Cliff Road and head east for 1.2 miles. Turn right at the park entrance sign at N. Hay Lake Road. You'll see the parking lot for the visitor center after about 0.6 mile. GPS: N44°47.17167' / W93°07.74000'

The Hike

Lebanon Hills Regional Park appears on a lot of "best of" lists in the Twin Cities. It's recognized for great mountain biking, great cross-country skiing, canoeing, and, of course, hiking. With five different trailheads to choose from, including the equestrian path, deciding where to start is much more difficult than choosing

There are many trails at Lebanon Hills, but numbered signposts like these make them easy to navigate. DAVID BAUR

Looking southwest near Cattail Lake's portage route DAVID BAUR

to visit in the first place. The visitor center trailhead is a good choice for first-timers. It's the easiest one to find, and its access to the center's information and creature comforts comes in handy. That's before considering that Schulze Lake provides a gorgeous introduction to the park. This twisty route begins there and heads northwest into the adjacent forests.

The vast trail network at Lebanon Hills means you'll be passing through more complex intersections than most hikes. Trails seem to spread out in every direction, making a map even more handy than usual. That said, this may be the most well-marked park featured in this book. With numbered intersections and very frequent maps and signage, you shouldn't have too much trouble finding your way, and there's always another route to get somewhere if you miss a turn.

Right from the start, your path heads uphill on an extremely wide trail. It's a rustic mix of grass and forest floor, but the incline is mostly gradual. It's enough to get your heart rate up if you're moving quickly, but it's not overly challenging.

> Be courteous of others. Many people visit natural areas for quiet, peace, and solitude, so avoid making loud noises and intruding on others' privacy.

By the time you're 0.7 mile in, you've already reached the highest point in the route, near a small picnic area, though the hike remains hilly throughout. Being uphill brings pleasant views as you draw closer to Holland Lake. You'll spy the blue of the lake peeking up at you through trees. It's a little taste of what you'll find if you decide to add the loop that leads to the Holland Lake Trailhead.

When you reach the western edge of the loop and double back, the dirt trail gets narrower, making you feel more embedded in the wilderness than the 1.5 mile or so as you skim the northern edge of O'Brien Lake. This section, part of the Voyageur Trek set of trails, is home to a gorgeous tree canopy, with elms, oak, and more. You'll likely spy some of Minnesota's roughly one billion ash trees, which are under dire threat from the invasive pest known as the emerald ash borer.

Between Cattail and Portage Lakes, you'll likely find dozens of leopard frogs enjoying the hike with you and maybe see a garter snake or two. The trail occasionally dips close to shorelines as you pass the portage connections for the canoe trails that link several of the bodies of water in the southwestern portion of the park. If it wasn't already obvious why Lebanon Hills is popular for canoeing, these lakes make it obvious. They are beautiful and make you feel as though you're somewhere more remote than you really are. If you can't make it to the Boundary Waters, this is a nice consolation. As you wind back toward the trailhead and come to the southwestern shores of Schulze Lake, it's pretty clear that you can't really go wrong at Lebanon Hills, no matter which paths you choose.

> As part of the efforts to demonstrate sustainability, the Lebanon Hills Visitor Center has a vegetative roof.

Miles and Directions

0.0   Start on the paved trail behind the visitor center building, across from the parking lot, along the northeast side of Schulze Lake and hike northwest toward trail marker #50.

0.2   At trail marker #40, take the right-hand path (northwest) and head uphill.

1.2   At marker #32, take the sharpest right (west) toward marker #29 and the Holland Lake Trailhead.

1.4   At marker #29, proceed through the intersection, heading southwest. Take the middle-left trail toward marker #24 for the Jensen Lake Trailhead along the

Lebanon Hills East

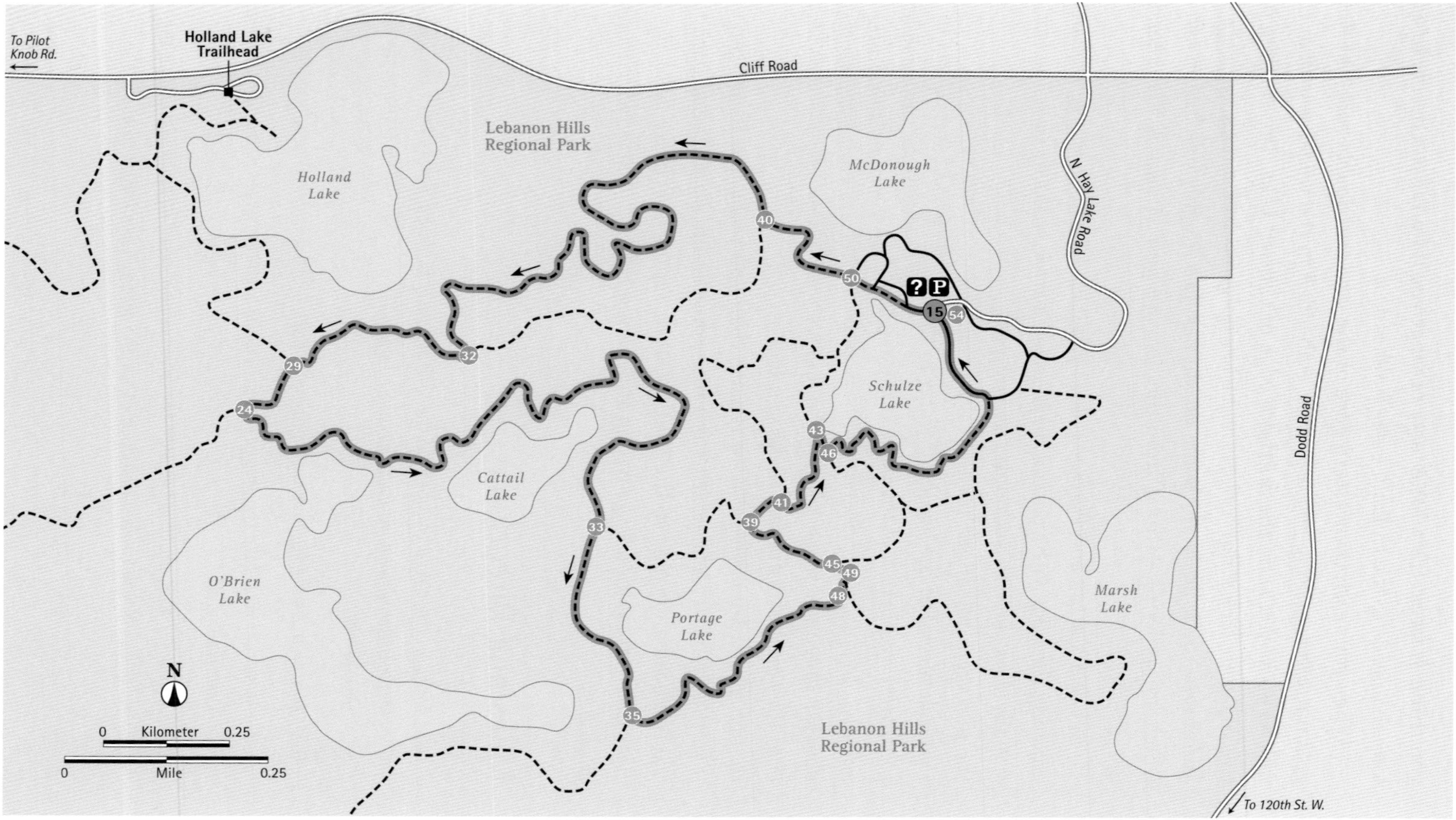

To Pilot Knob Rd.

Cliff Road

Holland Lake Trailhead

Holland Lake

Lebanon Hills Regional Park

McDonough Lake

N Hay Lake Road

Dodd Road

To 120th St. W.

Schulze Lake

Marsh Lake

Lebanon Hills Regional Park

Portage Lake

Cattail Lake

O'Brien Lake

40

50

15 54

?P

43

46

45 49

48

41

39

35

33

32

29

24

N

Kilometer   0   0.25

Mile   0   0.25

Voyageur Trek route. (*Option:* Turn right to add a loop to your northwest that passes near Holland Lake.)

1.5 At marker #24, turn left (east) toward marker #33 on the Voyageur Trek Trail.

2.6 At marker #33, turn right (south) toward marker #35.

2.8 Turn left (northeast) at marker #35, leaving the Voyageur Trek Trail and heading toward marker #48.

3.2 At marker #48, cross straight through the intersection toward marker #49 and then turn left (west) toward marker #45.

3.3 Now at marker #45, continue west toward marker #39.

3.4 At marker #39, turn right (northeast) toward marker #41, bearing northeast. Shortly thereafter choose the right-hand path for marker #43.

3.6 Bend right (east) near marker #46, circling around the southeastern shore of Schulze Lake.

3.9 Turn left (northwest) as you emerge from the unpaved trails and meet up with the paved trail leading toward the beach and visitor center.

4.1 Arrive at marker #54 for the visitor center trailhead.

Hike Information

Local Information: Explore Minnesota; (888) 847-4866; exploreminnesota.com

16 Afton State Park

Less than half an hour from Saint Paul, Afton State Park is proof positive that you don't have to travel far to get away. Across 20 miles of trails, you'll find everything from rugged climbs up steep ravines and along river bluffs to gentle strolls through prairie and oak savanna. When you've worn yourself out, head down to the long, slender beach to look out on the beautiful Saint Croix River and relax. Combining a variety of landscapes, spectacular views, and wildlife, Afton is a hiker's heaven.

Start: Trailhead north of the turnaround for the park road

Distance: 5.3-mile loop

Hiking time: About 2 hours

Difficulty: Strenuous due to two challenging climbs and descents on mostly rustic trails

Trail surface: Brief portions of blacktop, but mostly dirt, forest floor, and grass

Best season: Year-round

Other trail users: Equestrians and cyclists on designated trails

Canine compatibility: Dogs on leashes of not more than 6 feet permitted

Land status: Public Minnesota state park

Fees and permits: Parking permits required; both daily and annual permits available

Schedule: 8 a.m. to 10 p.m. daily

Trail contacts and maps: Afton State Park; (651) 436-5391; dnr.state.mn.us/state _parks/afton/index.html

Finding the trailhead: From I-94 near downtown Saint Paul, go 9 miles east to exit 253 for MN 95 S/CR 15/Manning Avenue. Take the exit and head south for 7 miles by turning right (east) onto Manning Avenue. Turn left (east) onto 70th Street S/Washington CR 20 and head east for 3.5 miles. At the intersection with Peller Avenue, continue straight to enter the park's main road and pass near the park office. Stay on that road for almost 2 miles until you reach the turnaround loop at its northern end. GPS: N44°51.33000' / W092°46.49333'

The Hike

Some parks are special because they're not well known or heavily traveled, and visiting them makes you feel like you know something everyone else doesn't. With nearly 200,000 annual visitors, Afton State Park is no secret, but that popularity is a testament to its enduring appeal. This route tackles several of the

Picnic tables up near this cabin are a good spot to grab some lunch. DAVID BAUR

northern trail sections, and there are opportunities to elongate your trip if you wish.

Begin by hiking north along the river, working your way downhill first. Be sure to stop at the lookout point near the stairs first for a preview of where you're headed. The trail along your descent can begin to be a little unclear and difficult to follow because you're passing through a confluence of many different trails and in close proximity to campgrounds. Just keep making your way straight north, and the path will get clearer.

When the trail levels out, it begins to trace the river on a ridge. You'll see bottomland forest below on your right and the edge of the bluffs to your left. Glimpses of the river sneak into view as the path draws closer to its edge, and the trail soon leads you down to the beach. It's not very wide, but it does stretch along pretty much the entire shore within the park.

Continuing northward from the beach, you're on the section called the North River Trail. The path you want is marked by a blue diamond and is open to both hikers and cyclists. Blue diamonds will help you stay on course throughout the hike.

Near the northern end of this first section, just before crossing the second of two small bridges, you can veer off the main course to follow a dirt trail into the woods to your west. This trail leads to a steep and very challenging uphill trek to reach the ridgetops above. If that sounds like more than you bargained for, stay

Afton's rustic trails are good fun but can be tricky. Watch your step! DAVID BAUR

on the main path. It's also steep and challenging, but the well-maintained trail eases the burden somewhat.

However you choose to ascend, the experience up top is remarkably different from the woods and ravines below. You'll begin the Prairie Loop by entering an open field with scarcely a hint to suggest there are steep cliffs, a river, or just about anything else nearby. Where moments ago you were in deep forest, now you're in open prairie and oak savanna, with milkweed and tall grasses replacing the tree canopy. The blue diamonds on trail posts continue to guide your way, but it's almost like entering an entirely different park.

The Prairie Loop is a welcome respite after the grueling climb to get there. It's a bridle trail as well, with some dips here and there, but it's a mostly flat ring around the ridges of the northern half of the park. The flip side is that this entire stretch is exposed, so be prepared if you're visiting on a hot day. Drink plenty of water, reapply sunscreen, and so on. There are also a couple of shelters where you can rest or have a snack.

> If at all possible, camp in established sites. If there are none, then camp in an unobtrusive area at least 200 feet (70 paces) from the nearest water source.

(*Options:* If you're looking to extend your hike, the Prairie Loop has a couple of extra sections you can add, or you can venture downhill on the west side to tackle the Trout Brook Loop. Also on the western side of the Prairie Loop, you'll find occasional breaks in the foliage with vistas out over the surrounding ravines. It's a reminder that the whole area is elevated relative to its surroundings. On the southern edge there's a lookout point toward the slopes at Afton Alps, which provide a sense of scale.)

Finishing up the Prairie Loop, you'll head back downhill through another ravine similar to your earlier climb. The route then bends south and crosses Trout Brook, where, if you look to your right, you'll find yourself looking up at those same Afton Alps ski slopes. Admire how far you've come before you tackle one last doozy of a climb back to the trailhead.

Miles and Directions

0.0   Start at the trailhead north of the turnaround for the park road and hike north, heading downhill on the North River Trail. Stick to the central path, avoiding any branches to the left and right as you head downhill.

Afton State Park

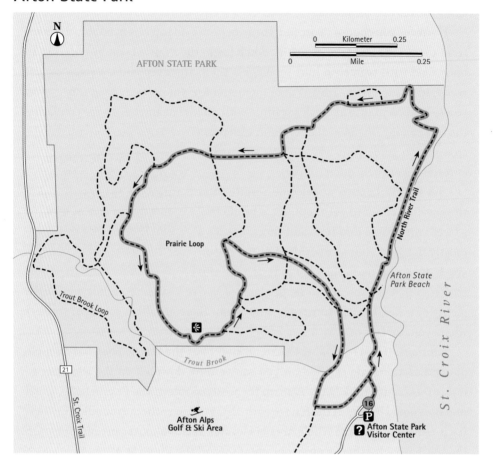

1.0 Continue northeast as you cross a wooden bridge. The trail then heads steeply uphill north and west. (*Option:* Just before crossing the bridge, head downhill on the dirt trail to your left [west]. It offers a fun and more challenging climb up to the Prairie Loop on a rugged trail.)

1.5 Continue straight (west) through the trail intersection that heads downhill to your left or onto a small loop to your right.

1.8 Turn right (west) at the next multi-way intersection.

2.0 Turn right (west) again at another four-way intersection and onto the Prairie Loop. (*Bailout:* Continue straight ahead at this intersection to hike downhill through another ravine and meet up with the trail directions beginning around 4.2 miles.)

2.3 Continue straight (west) at another four-way intersection. (*Side trip:* Turn right [north] to add an additional segment to the Prairie Loop or to connect to the Trout Brook Loop.)

2.6 Just as the trail turns south, stay to your left (south) at the three-way intersection.

2.8 Continue straight (south) along the ridge as another trail enters on your right.

3.6 Your trail begins to turn back north. Ignore all trail intersections until milepoint 4.0.

4.0 Turn right (east) and downhill through a ravine, leaving the Prairie Loop.

4.2 Stay on your current trail as it bends south, ignoring the trails that link into it until you reach 4.9 miles after crossing Trout Brook.

4.9 Turn left (east) on a mix of dirt and paved road. It's another very steep climb.

5.2 Turn right (south) to head farther uphill. The trail merges with the web of trails from the beginning of the hike.

5.3 Arrive back at the trailhead.

Hike Information

Local Information: Explore Minnesota; (888) 847-4866; exploreminnesota.com

ROAD CYCLING

The Twin Cities—Minneapolis in particular—are frequently ranked the best in the United States for their cycling infrastructure. As of 2015, Minneapolis has 129 miles of on-street bikeways and 97 miles of off-street bikeways. The city of Saint Paul counts 120 miles between off-street paths (79) and roadways with striped bike lanes (41). That's only counting inside the respective cities. A number of the routes featured in this book extend to the surrounding suburbs and exurbs. Truth is, one could easily connect all of the routes featured in this book without a hitch. But because most riders can't fit in a couple hundred miles in an afternoon, I've broken up the routes based on popularity and what most would consider a reasonable distance. Regardless of how you decide to tackle these rides, you'll have to agree that they're some of the best riding in the country.

Not only is this region nationally recognized for its commitment to cycling, but Minneapolis is no stranger to international rankings that put the city in the same conversation as the cycling meccas of Europe.

Cruising along Mississippi River Boulevard is a serene section of the St. Paul Grand Round. STEVE JOHNSON

It's also the best way to get a taste of the city and nature in one adventure without ever setting foot in a car. While living in the Minneapolis neighborhood of Whittier, I could step right outside, hop on a bike, and be off on a number of routes. Dense forests that are typically far removed from an urban environment were a short 10 miles from home.

Now a brief explainer. These road rides are a mix of city streets, paths, and suburban/exurban trails composed of crushed limestone. Always be sure you have the right tires for your ride. Depending on when you ride, you're bound to find both ends of the spectrum in terms of bike traffic. Naturally warm, sunny weekends will yield more cyclists. If you're out for an early morning workout ride in the middle of the week in April, you might be by yourself for the most part. Point is, be mindful of other cyclists. Don't be that rider who blows by cyclists on crowded park paths. Slow down or hop on the road if you want to gain a little speed. More often than not the paved road routes will have on-road alternatives that parallel the cycling paths. The crushed limestone trails, however, rarely trace alongside a paved road, so do respect that not everyone is up for dressing in Lycra and hitting the bike like they're about to climb the Koppenberg in Belgium's Ronde van Vlaanderen.

Finally, do be mindful of distracted drivers. Take all the precautions you can to make yourself visible, but any regular cyclist knows that's not always enough. America's roadways are still largely populated with Darwin Award nominees who will text and drive. Though the Twin Cities are to be celebrated for their cycling infrastructure, I anecdotally noticed less attentiveness from drivers in the surrounding suburbs and exurbs. In fact, I got hit by a car during the production of this book, but more on that later.

Be smart, be safe, be respectful, and enjoy some of the best cycling in all of these United States.

BIKE SHOPS

Minneapolis

Angry Catfish Bicycle + Coffee Bar: 4208 S. 28th Ave., Minneapolis 55406; (612) 722-1538; angrycatfishbicycle.com

Charlie's Tangletown Bike Shop: 322 W. 48th St., Minneapolis 55409; (612) 259-8180; tangletownbikeshop.com

Erik's: 2800 Lyndale Ave. S, Ste. 1, Minneapolis 55408; 612-872-8600; www.eriksbikeshop.com

Flanders Brothers Cycle: 2707 Lyndale Ave. S, Minneapolis 55408; (612) 872-6994; flandersbros.com

Freewheel Bike Midtown Bike Center: 2834 10th Ave. S, Minneapolis 55407; (612) 238-4447; freewheelbikecenter.com

The Hub Bike Co-op: 3020 Minnehaha Ave., Minneapolis 55406; (612) 729-0437; thehubbikecoop.org

One On One Bicycle Studio: 117 N. Washington Ave., Minneapolis 55401; (612) 371-9565; oneononebike.com.

Penn Cycle: 710 W. Lake St., Minneapolis 55408; (612) 822-2228; penncycle.com

Perennial Cycle: 3342 Hennepin Ave. S, Minneapolis 55408; (612) 827-8000; perennialcycle.com

Sunrise Cyclery: 2901 Blaisdell Ave. S, Minneapolis 55408; (612) 824-6144; sunrisecyclerympls.com.

Two Wheels Bike Shop: 1014 W. 27th St., Minneapolis 55408; (612) 735-7345

Venture North Bikes: 1830 Glenwood Ave., Minneapolis 55405; (612) 377-3029; venturenorthbwc.org

Saint Paul

Capital Deals: 710 Smith Ave. S, Saint Paul 55107; (651) 222-8380; capitaldealsonline.com

Cycles for Change: 712 University Ave. W, Saint Paul 55104; (651) 222-2080; cyclesforchange.org

Express Bike Shop: 1158 Selby Ave., Saint Paul 55104; (651) 644-9660; exbike.com

Grand Performance: 1938 Grand Ave., Saint Paul 55105; (651) 699-2640; gpbicycles.com

Lowertown Bike Shop: 214 E. 4th St., #160, Saint Paul 55101; (651) 222-0775; lowertownbikeshop.com

Now Bikes & Fitness: 75 N. Snelling Ave., Saint Paul 55104; (651) 644-2534; nowbikes-fitness.com

Seven Spokes: 1044 Cleveland Ave. S, Saint Paul 55116; (651) 698-2453; sevenspokesbikeshop.com

17 Cedar Lake to Midtown and Hiawatha Ramble

This combination of commuter favorites makes for a great spin around downtown Minneapolis and its inner-ring suburbs and neighborhoods.

Start: Cedar Lake LRT Regional Trail behind Target Field near the Target Field Station and Rail Platform

Distance: 21-mile loop

Riding time: About 1.5 hours

Terrain and trail surface: Paved and mostly flat

Traffic and hazards: These trails are open only to human power and are used mostly by training and commuting cyclists. However, walkers and runners also use the trail, and it is best to be courteous and give them the right of way when encountered. This route does cross vehicular traffic at certain intersections, so do take caution.

Things to see: Target Field, rail lines, meadows, Mississippi River

Getting there: **By car:** Take Washington Avenue from Minneapolis and turn left past Dunn Brothers Coffee North Loop toward the Cedar Lake LRT Regional Trail entrance. Coming from Saint Paul, take I-94 W for about 11 miles toward Minneapolis. Take Washington Avenue and turn left at Dunn Brothers Coffee North Loop toward a parking lot next to Cedar Lake Trail and the Target Field Station and Rail Platform. GPS: N44°58.595' / W93° 16.368'

The Ride

This ride, perhaps more than any other in the book, shows just how impressive a cycling network the Twin Cities have. We begin on the Cedar Lake LRT Regional Trail, looping around inner-ring suburb Saint Louis Park, cutting through the southern end of the city on the Midtown Greenway, and then rolling north to the Mississippi River on the Hiawatha Bike Trail along the train line of the same name.

That's 20 miles of connected bike infrastructure completely separated from vehicular traffic. That means no close calls with dullards trying to text and navigate dense city streets or steamy farts from each and every muffler passing by.

The thundering Mississippi River as seen from the Stone Arch Bridge in downtown Minneapolis JOE BAUR

Minneapolis is yours to enjoy on two wheels, and it's an example the rest of the country would be smart to follow.

For no particular reason, I opted to do the loop counterclockwise, starting right outside Target Field where the Minnesota Twins attempt to play something resembling stickball. The beautiful thing about the Cedar Lake Trail is that you get a nice mixture of urban and something resembling what the city may have looked like before there was, y'know, a city. I'm talking about tall grasses and trees—*actual trees!*—that will make you feel as if you're in parkland and not in the middle of Minneapolis.

I first had the privilege of rolling on this route years ago when my brother moved to the area and bought a home in Saint Louis Park. A trail entrance was right around the corner from his house, so I borrowed a bike and headed downtown. I was, and remain, amazed at how incredible this piece of cycling infrastructure is.

The Cedar Lake Trail wraps around the southern edge of the city before turning into the Midtown Greenway about 13 miles into the ride, though it's worth noting that you'll run into Excelsior Boulevard about 8 miles into the ride. Across the street is the Depot Coffee House, where you can grab a snack or even tune up your bike if you need a little more air in those tires. If you do cross over, you'll also notice that the Minnesota River Bluffs Trail picks up alongside the Depot and the adjacent train tracks. This is a ride for another day, or it can be combined with the Minnesota River Bluffs to Lake Minnetonka Loop Ramble to add another 28.5 miles to the ride.

Now back to the Midtown Greenway, which essentially is an urban freeway for cyclists that's also used by joggers and walkers alike. This, combined with the Cedar Lake Trail, is why Minneapolis is routinely crowned the best cycling city in the United States, and people are throwing money for the opportunity to live in the new condos and apartments that have since gone up around the Greenway. I, for one, am envious.

The Midtown Greenway cuts west to east across the southern end of the city (passing the Freewheel Bike Center along the way) for about 4 miles before hitting the Hiawatha Bike Trail, though the Greenway does continue a bit farther east to River Parkway. As the name suggests, the Hiawatha Bike Trail follows the rail line of the same name, making for some cool views of the city when a train passes by and the skyline is in the backdrop.

The Hiawatha Bike Trail gets you back into the heart of Minneapolis with the goal of connecting back to the Cedar Lake Trail to finish the loop. For a more scenic ride, I opted to get off the trail after about 1.5 miles at 11th Avenue South and worked my way north to River Parkway along the Mississippi River. Then, it's

MIDTOWN GREENWAY

Minneapolis's Midtown Greenway might just be the most impressive piece of cycling infrastructure I've seen in the United States—or even the world. In effect, it's a bikes-only highway with on-ramps and exits just like we've seen with automobile expressways. But unlike those vehicular highways that have been regrettably carved across the United States, the Midtown Greenway is pleasant.

The 5.5-mile-long path skates along a former railroad corridor in the southern end of Minneapolis, complete with a pedestrian lane for runners and walkers. The Midtown Greenway Coalition (midtowngreenway.org) is the grassroots organization that worked to advocate its installation, connecting the western Chain of Lakes to the light rail line and the paths along the Mississippi River. Like anything you'd find for cars, the Midtown Greenway is open 24/7 and is plowed throughout the winter for the thousands of cyclists who use the path year-round.

Cedar Lake to Midtown to Hiawatha Ramble

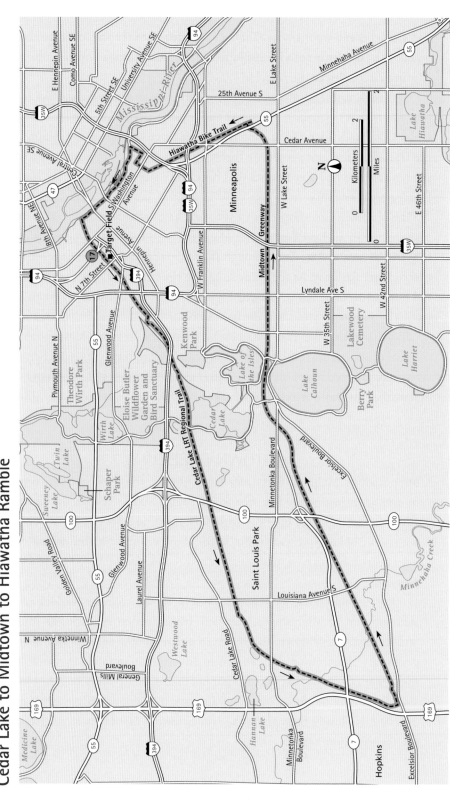

just a mile ride along the river before connecting with the Cedar Lake Trail again with a left turn, cycling south for less than a mile before returning to the start.

Miles and Directions

0.0   Start on the Cedar Lake Trail near N. 5th Street, slightly northeast of Target Field along the rail tracks. Ride the trail southwest toward Target Field.

8.4   Arrive at Excelsior Boulevard. Across the street is the Depot Coffee House, where you can stop for a snack or pump up your tires if they feel a bit flat. Otherwise, continue on the Cedar Lake Trail as the path turns east along Excelsior Boulevard.

8.8   Cross Jackson Avenue N to continue on the Cedar Lake Trail.

12.5   Trail turns into the Midtown Greenway. Follow the path as it cuts east across the city for just over 4 miles, when you'll reach the Martin Olav Sabo Bridge. Climb the bridge, descend on the other side, and take a sharp left (northwest) onto the Hiawatha Trail parallel to the train tracks.

18.6   Exit the trail onto 11th Avenue S. Pass Washington Avenue and turn right (southeast) onto S. 2nd Street for 2 blocks. Then take a left onto S. 13th Avenue for a short distance until it runs into W. River Parkway.

19.1   Turn left (west) onto W. River Parkway. Continue cycling along the Mississippi River until you reach the Cedar Lake Trail.

20.4   Turn left (west) onto the Cedar Lake Trail.

21.0   Arrive back at the start.

18 Dakota to Minnetonka Loop Ramble

It's mostly crushed limestone trail as you loop around Lake Minnetonka, connecting the Dakota Rail Regional Trail to the southern Lake Minnetonka LRT Regional Trail in Excelsior for a 20-mile ride west of the Twin Cities.

Start: Wayzata Beach Park

Distance: 20-mile loop

Riding time: About 1.5 hours

Terrain and trail surface: Aggregate trail and paved path with short jaunts on the road

Traffic and hazards: These trails are popular with recreational cyclists, especially on warm weekends, so gauge bike traffic and pedal at a reasonable, safe speed. The trail portions are also constructed with crushed limestone, so ensure you have proper tires that won't leave you stranded with a flat. Finally, there are a couple of sections where you jump on the road. Do be mindful of distracted drivers.

Things to see: Wayzata Beach, Lake Minnetonka, Excelsior

Getting there: From I-394 W, drive west toward Wayzata and continue onto US 12 W. Keep left to stay on US 12 W for 1.8 miles. Then, take the exit for CR 101 S/ Wayzata. Take Wayzata Boulevard E and Barry Avenue toward Grove Lane E. Continue to Bushaway Road/Gleason Lake Drive. Use the two right lanes to turn right toward and onto Wayzata Boulevard E. In about a mile, turn left on Barry Avenue and continue to Grove Lane E. Wayzata Beach will be directly ahead of you. GPS: N44°58.13297' / W93°31.15135'

The Ride

Wayzata Beach and Lake Minnetonka in general are popular weekend getaways during the warmer, humid summer months. It also makes for a logical start to this 20-mile loop that connects both the Dakota Rail Regional Trail and the Lake Minnetonka LRT Regional Trail. It's worth mentioning, though, that the Luce Line Regional Trail is a short mile or so away on the northern edge of Wayzata. In fact, when recording these routes for the book, I connected the 12-mile Luce Line ride starting from Theodore Wirth Park to Wayzata and completed that loop around Lake Minnetonka. That turned this 20-mile ride into 42 miles by the time I doubled back to Theodore Wirth, plus a little more to get home in Whittier.

A cyclist rolls over the Dakota Rail Regional Trail. JOE BAUR

It's worth repeating that this is precisely what makes cycling in the Twin Cities so utterly fantastic. You will never fall short of options when it comes to cycling, and you'll almost always have the option to hit a path or trail if you're not quite comfortable with mixing yourself among cars. In fact, I completely understand when some folks tell me they don't feel comfortable on the road. Any regular cyclist, for sport or commuting, can recount a number of close calls with distracted drivers. I'm no different, but luckily I had never actually been hit by a car. That is, until this very ride.

Anyone with a quick glance of Wayzata Beach can see why so many would make the trip out here on a summer day. Clear skies, a nice breeze off the lake, and a pleasant patch of sand are at the start of the trail. The paved Dakota Rail Regional Trail begins just off the beach near Peavey Lane, and you stick to it for about 6 miles, hitting a nice bridge that crosses over the water near Minnetonka Beach right before you turn off the trail. This is when you'll get some time on the road and mix with vehicular traffic. If you don't feel comfortable on the road, another option is to continue on the Dakota Rail Regional Trail for another 7 miles. That'll get you to the full 13 paved miles on this particular trail, and you can always turn back to Wayzata and hop on the Luce Line to get back to Minneapolis.

If you can stand the cars, it'll be a left onto Shadywood Road, which quickly turns into Manitou Road as you wind through Crescent Beach and Tonka Bay. After about 3 miles, you'll run into the southern edge of this loop by turning left (east) onto Lake Minnetonka LRT Trail, an aggregate trail that extends 15 miles in total if starting farther west in Victoria, Minnesota. In this loop, you'll get about 6.5 miles on this beautiful trail that cuts through small towns and what at times seems like dense forest. It's at the 15.5-mile marker that you'll come to Tonkawood Road; turn left to get back toward the water and the start at Wayzata Beach.

Now remember when I said I had never been hit by a car until this very ride? I also mentioned earlier that, at least anecdotally, drivers farther from the Twin Cities are more distracted and drive larger vehicles. Because of road design, they also drive much faster. All of these things came into play against me on Tonkawood Road, which ironically is less than 0.5 mile of a 20-mile ride. Ninety-nine times out of a hundred, I'm sure it'd be a quick straightaway before continuing onward to more scenic portions of the ride.

I approached the stop sign at the end of Tonkawood Road, where you then turn left very briefly onto Minnetonka Boulevard for less than 0.3 mile, connecting to the much calmer Fairchild Avenue for a pleasant cool down back to Wayzata Beach. The vehicular traffic on Minnetonka Boulevard moves fast, and there's a hump in the road going from Tonkawood to Minnetonka that makes it difficult for a cyclist to get the momentum back. Drivers on Minnetonka trying to turn left onto Tonkawood stare straight ahead to make sure they themselves don't get T-boned, and they hit the gas whenever there's a gap. That's precisely what happened with a rather large white vehicle, except it kept turning directly into my lane and hit me straight on as I continued waiting at the stop sign.

Fortunately, I was perfectly fine, remarkably so considering I was just met head-on by thousands of pounds of metal. The woman behind the wheel was also as kind as one can hope from a driver who just hit a defenseless cyclist. She looked like Hallmark's grumpy Maxine character, sunglasses and all, but with a polar opposite temperament. (That's "Minnesota nice" for you.) But considering she kept insisting that she never saw me despite my video evidence (that's right, I was recording), which showed she went right into me, I left hopeful that somebody would be taking her license away from her. Or maybe, as so often happens, it'll be determined that the driver's exam she took half a century ago is good enough to keep her on the road.

Dakota to Minnetonka Loop Ramble

After leaving my information with the police officer, I was allowed to continue onward and finish the ride along Grays Bay Boulevard and on a small bridge over a small corner of the lake that cuts back up north to McGinty Road W. A left turn there takes you over to Lake Street E and right back to where we started at Wayzata Beach Park.

Miles and Directions

0.0   Start at Wayzata Beach Park and pedal west on Peavey Lane, taking the first right (north) onto Peavey Road, followed immediately by a left (west) onto the Dakota Rail Regional Trail.

6.0   Turn left (southeast) onto Shadywood Road.

7.0   Shadywood Road becomes Manitou Road for the remaining 2 miles until you hit the Lake Minnetonka LRT Regional Trail.

9.0   Turn left (east) onto the Lake Minnetonka LRT Regional Trail for 6.5 miles until you reach Tonkawood Road.

15.5   Turn left (north) onto Tonkawood Road.

15.9   Turn left (west) onto Minnetonka Boulevard followed by a quick right onto Fairchild Avenue.

16.8   Turn right (north) onto Grays Bay Boulevard, pedaling through Minnehaha Creek Headwaters and onto a wooden bridge that connects with Crosby Cove.

17.6   Continue straight (north) on Crosby Cove until you reach the intersection with Crosby Road, where you'll turn right (east) and follow it as it bends to the left (north).

17.9   Turn left (northwest) onto McGinty Road W for a little over a mile.

19.1   Turn right (north) onto E. Circle Drive, where you'll hit a roundabout. Follow it counterclockwise and turn onto Lake Street E, pedaling west.

19.9   Turn left onto Grove Lane E for the final 0.1 mile that takes you right back to Wayzata Beach Park.

20.0   Arrive back at Wayzata Beach Park.

19 Luce Line to Wayzata Beach Park Ramble

The Luce Line State and Regional Trail stretches over 70 miles from Minneapolis's Theodore Wirth Park to the tiny town of Cosmos in central Minnesota. Conquering the entire trail is certainly an option for overnight riders, but here we tackle a modest 12 miles of the trail to the logical stopping point of Wayzata Beach Park, where you can continue onto the Dakota Rail Regional Trail or double back to Theodore Wirth Park in Minneapolis.

Start: Luce Line Regional Trail trailhead at Theodore Wirth Park

Distance: 24-mile out and back

Riding time: About 2 hours

Terrain and trail surface: Paved and mostly flat

Traffic and hazards: These trails are open only to human power and are used mostly by training and commuting cyclists. However, walkers and runners also use the trail, and it is best to be courteous and give them the right of way when encountered. This route does cross vehicular traffic at certain intersections, so do take caution.

Things to see: Theodore Wirth Park, Wayzata Beach Park, Lake Minnetonka

Getting there: Take Plymouth Avenue N west from Minneapolis until it ends at Theodore Wirth Parkway. Turn left onto Theodore Wirth Parkway and pass a parking lot immediately on your right for the golf course and Winter Recreation Area. The trailhead for the Luce Line Regional Trail is 0.3 mile farther south on Theodore Wirth Parkway on the right. GPS: N44°59.38330' / W93°19.60848'

The Ride

The Luce Line State Trail begins 9 miles west of Theodore Wirth Park in the Minneapolis suburb of Plymouth; but as this book is written largely in the spirit of the influx of Americans returning to cities, I've opted to start this ride in the city with the Luce Line *Regional* Trail out of the park. Plus, if you've ridden the Minneapolis Grand Round, you've been in Theodore Wirth Park and already know it's a beautiful side of the city.

The Luce Line trails in this ride are paved and easy to navigate if you can follow signs. The trailhead at Theodore Wirth starts off with a dense forest ride typical of the Twin Cities' parks systems. Eventually it does space out a bit (and becomes less scenic) when you get into the suburbs, where you'll find more

LUCE LINE

Like many trails in the Twin Cities, the Luce Line is steeped in rail history. The story goes that one W. L. Luce, alongside his son, E. D. Luce, incorporated the Electric Short Line Railroad Company in 1908. The plan at the time was to construct a railroad from Minneapolis out to Brookings, South Dakota, in hopes of linking a number of farming communities that went unserved by rail.

Construction began in 1913 with 8 miles of track that went into operation between the Minneapolis city limits at Glenwood and Parkers Lake. This continued the following year with tracks added along the northern shore of Lake Minnetonka and farther west into Winsted. The railroad reached all the way out to Hutchinson by the end of 1915.

However, the Luce Line had a late start in railroad history and was constructed along the perimeter of the towns it purported to serve. Because much of the land they wanted to travel was already settled, they were left going over that which was not suitable for farming, like wetlands. Still, they were able to gain business and even market the line to tourists and local vacationers who wanted to visit the popular resorts on Medicine Lake and Lake Minnetonka.

Moving ahead a bit, the line lasted well into the 1950s, but other forms of transportation made the railroad unprofitable by the 1960s. The Luce Line was formally abandoned in 1970, and talks of converting it to a recreation trail began just three years later.

suburban office space and wide roads than trees. The beauty returns, however, as you get closer to Medicine Lake and the trailhead for the Medicine Lake Regional Trail—another ride for another day. From the Medicine Lake junction, the ride is as straightforward as straight can be as it cuts through Plymouth, where the regional trail uneventfully becomes the state trail.

Eleven miles into the ride, you'll come to N. Ferndale Road. Of course the Luce Line trail keeps going west into central Minnesota for another 60-some miles, but we're turning left and heading to the beach. Ferndale continues for about another mile until you just about run out of road and pedal onto Wayzata Beach Park. Note that this area can become insanely crowded during the warm summer months, so try and time your visit just right. If you're flexible, it's a bit more peaceful to get there on an early weekday morning.

Luce Line to Wayzata Beach Park Ramble

N Dowling Avenue

Bottineau Boulevard

Theodore Wirth Park

Lake Calhoun

Cedar Lake

Minnetonka Boulevard

Excelsior Boulevard

Twin Lake

Wirth Lake

Sweeney Lake

Schaper Park

Douglas Drive N

Glenwood Avenue

Laurel Avenue

Saint Louis Park

Louisiana Avenue S

Winnetka Avenue N

Golden Valley Road

Golden Valley

Westwood Lake

Cedar Lake Road

N 36th Avenue

27th Avenue N

Medicine Lake

Medicine Lake

Hannan Lake

Hopkins

Clifton E. French Regional Park

Hopkins Crossroad

Northwest Boulevard

Plymouth

Plymouth Road

Minnetonka

Minnetonka Boulevard

Rockford Road

Olsen Memorial Highway

Xenium Lane N

Parkers Lake

Wayzata

McGinty Road W

Vicksburg Lane N

Luce Line State Trail

Gleason Lake

Grays Bay

Libbs Lake

Dunkirk Lane N

Medina Road

Mooney Lake

Hadley Lake

Boulevard E

Lake Street E

Wayzata Beach Park

Wayzata Beach Park

Wayzata Bay

Holy Name Lake

Hunter Drive

N Ferndale Road

Wayzata

Lake Minnetonka

N

Kilometers

Miles

From a wooden bridge crossing over swampy-looking Gleason Lake on the Luce Line trail JOE BAUR

From Ferndale, you may notice that you've passed the Dakota Rail Regional Trail. Hopping on this trail for a jaunt farther west or to connect to the Lake Minnetonka LRT Regional Trail for a loop around Lake Minnetonka is an option. For the purposes of this chapter, you're heading right back where you came from to end the ride at Theodore Wirth Park at an even 24 miles.

Miles and Directions

0.0 Start at the Luce Line trailhead in Theodore Wirth Park.

4.0 The trail crosses Boone Avenue N and takes a quick left to run parallel to Plymouth Ave N on the southern end of the road.

4.6 After pedaling underneath US 169, the trail crosses Plymouth Avenue to the north side of the street and continues northwest along 13th Avenue N.

5.0 Arrive at the Medicine Lake Regional Trail junction, where you can add another ride from this book or continue west on the Luce Line.

11.1 The Luce Line continues west, but we're turning left (south) onto Ferndale Road N.

11.9 Turn left (east) onto Grove Lane E toward the beach.

12.0 End at Wayzata Beach Park. When ready, double back to the trailhead at Theodore Wirth Park.

20 Minneapolis Grand Round Cruise

There are over 100 miles of Grand Round trails that surround the city, so needless to say that this route connecting a number of the trails into a loop around Minneapolis offers a diverse look at the area.

Start: South end of the Stone Arch Bridge

Distance: 40-mile loop

Riding time: 2.5 to 4 hours

Terrain and trail surface: Paved and mostly flat

Traffic and hazards: These trails are open only to human power and are used mostly by training and commuting cyclists. However, walkers and runners also use the trail, and it is best to be courteous and give them the right of way when encountered. This route does cross vehicular traffic at certain intersections, so do take caution.

Things to see: The Chain of Lakes, Mississippi River, Stone Arch Bridge

Getting there: By car: From Minneapolis, drive north to W. River Parkway. A parking lot is just west of Portland Avenue on the north side of W. River Parkway near the Stone Arch Bridge.

From Saint Paul, take I-94 E for about 9 miles toward Minneapolis. Take exit 234B toward 5th Street. Turn right on 11th Avenue S, followed quickly by a left onto S. Washington Avenue. In less than 0.5 mile, turn right onto Portland Avenue S, followed shortly thereafter by a left onto W. River Parkway. The parking lot will be on your right. GPS: N44 58.513" / W 93 15.338"

The Ride

One of the cons of writing a book based in a city you live in only vicariously is that you have to part from your significant other. Luckily, my wife, Melanie, enjoys the Twin Cities as much as any human with proper tastes would and visited me during the writing of this book. Originally our plan was to go with a paddle, but the powers that be deemed that there would be no oars or kayaks in our immediate future.

But I had a book to write and an audience (you, dear reader) counting on me to make use of the gorgeous, sunny day to complete another chapter for *Best Outdoor Adventures Near Minneapolis and Saint Paul*. Luckily the answer was obvious, thanks to a couple of extra bikes at my brother's then-downtown apartment. Unfortunately for Melanie, it was single-speed urban commuter—not quite the

Rolling around the Chain of Lakes with the Minneapolis skyline coming into view JOE BAUR

quick-moving cross-country ride I had from One on One Bicycle Studio. There were also no clips, meaning anything resembling an incline had to be conquered with a mixture of previously gained momentum and pure up-and-down pounding of the legs. (New cyclists might not yet appreciate just how helpful having clips is. It's like doubling your power, especially on a climb.)

So we were off on the most obvious route given our location in downtown Minneapolis—the Minneapolis Grand Round, 40 miles of pristine asphalt and paved trail around the Mill City.

We started the route at one of my favorite points in the whole region, right at the architecturally stunning Stone Arch Bridge. Cycling (or walking, for that matter) over the Stone Arch Bridge always leaves me conflicted. I love it in the moment, but I often lament in retrospect that such bridges catering exclusively to pedestrians and cyclists are a rarity in this country. Then again, that's one of the many reasons why the Twin Cities are so popular with cyclists of all kinds.

Crossing over the Mississippi River, we pedaled north–northeast and hopped onto some trail separated from the road. Things take an industrial turn in these parts, with wider roads and smaller office buildings. Unfortunately we had a bit of a scary moment when a city garbage truck narrowly missed hitting Melanie as it turned left into a driveway and we were pedaling north. Melanie swerved out of the way, and we yelled obscenities, as one does when nearly plastered by a multi-ton machine. Surprisingly, the driver—a shorter, middle-aged man—stopped the truck immediately and jumped out of the front seat.

"Come here," he shouted, motioning toward me with his hand reaching toward something in his chest pocket.

The moment was so uncharacteristic to the Twin Cities, where the usual stereotype is a harmless person who might offer profuse apologies and eat something Scandinavian that would stop a healthy heart.

Obviously I refused to engage, being the respectable adult that I am. Instead we hopped back on our bikes and continued north as the little luddite muttered some expletive toward cyclists in general.

Neither of us were harmed or all that shaken by the incident. Rather, I was downright dumbfounded to find *that guy* exists in the Twin Cities—the cycling capital of the United States. *That guy* being the typical motorist we cyclists find in almost any other American city who would rather risk lives than drive safely.

RAILS-TO-TRAILS

There's a movement called rails-to-trails across the United States that aims to convert disused railways to cycling and walking paths. It's the cool thing to do now, but Minneapolis was doing it long before it became a hot topic in urban areas.

The Stone Arch Bridge is an early example and remains one of the more impressive additions to the country's trail network. The bridge opened as part of the Great Northern Railway in 1883, costing an astonishing $650,000. That's $16.5 million in today's dollars. Then that sad time period in American history happened when we moved away from trains and toward private automobiles, and the last passenger train crossed the Stone Arch Bridge in 1978.

Luckily the bridge was already on the National Register of Historic Places, so it didn't get knocked down or converted into a highway. Instead, the Hennepin County Regional Railroad Authority bought it in 1989 (transferred to the Minnesota Department of Transportation a few years later) and started the process of converting it into a cycling and walking path. The project was completed in 1994 by the Minneapolis Park & Recreation Board and remains one of the most popular attractions in the city for its views of the Mississippi River and its ability to let people pleasantly cross the city by foot or bike.

That guy who berates cyclists for simply existing and threatens them with thousands of pounds of metal.

So it wasn't a great start to the ride, but our situation vastly improved as we continued west on the northern end of the loop back through urban territory that felt more comfortable to ride in. This took us over the mighty Mississippi River and past the southern end of North Mississippi Regional Park as our path cut through Webber Park. (Minneapolis has a ton of parks, in case you couldn't tell.)

> Rechargeable (reusable) batteries reduce one source of toxic garbage.

Shortly after Webber Park, we hopped onto Victory Memorial Parkway for a green leafy ride south through Victory Memorial Regional Park and Theodore Wirth Park consecutively before linking up with the Chain of Lakes. With perfect weather, we were in no hurry to cut the ride short, so we added a quick 3-mile loop around the Lake of the Isles before continuing down the western edges of Lake Calhoun and Lake Harriet.

From there it was a breeze of a ride along Minnehaha Creek and its surrounding parks on the southern portion of the loop, connecting with W. River Parkway on the eastern edge of the route. Typically River Parkway gets you all the way back to Stone Arch, but some construction took us on a small detour down to Riverside Avenue before reconnecting to River Parkway. Then, it was just a short jaunt before finishing our 40-mile ride back at the Stone Arch Bridge.

Miles and Directions

0.0 Start at the southern end of the Stone Arch Bridge and cycle north across it. After the bridge, turn left (north) onto SE 6th Avenue for about 0.5 mile and turn right (east) onto SE 8th Street, followed by a quick left (north) onto SE 10th Avenue.

1.5 Make a quick turn right (east) onto SE Como Avenue. Stay on Como for just a handful of blocks before turning left (north) onto SE 18th Avenue.

2.1 A separated bike path appears on the right just after some train tracks that you can cycle on if you wish. Continue parallel to NE Stinson Boulevard until New Brighton Boulevard.

3.2 Turn right (northeast) onto New Brighton Boulevard or to continue on the bike path.

4.0 Turn left (northwest) onto Saint Anthony Parkway. Stay on Saint Anthony for about 5 miles until you reach the Mississippi River.

Minneapolis Grand Round Cruise

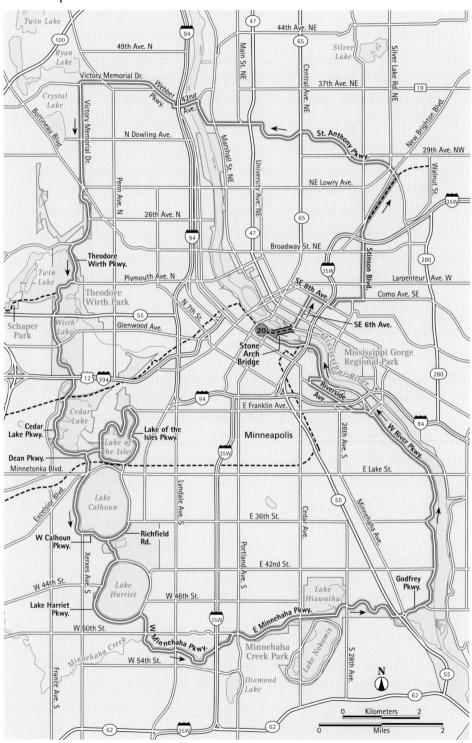

9.3   Turn left (west) onto N. 42nd Avenue over the Mississippi River. After passing the river and I-94, turn right (north) on N. Lyndale Avenue and take the first left (west) onto Webber Parkway. Stay on this road as it becomes Victory Memorial Drive.

11.5   Victory Memorial Drive will turn south. Continue on the road or the adjacent path. This road will eventually change its name to Theodore Wirth Parkway, which you'll stay on through the park and golf course of the same name for another 2 miles.

17.0   The road's name changes to Cedar Lake Parkway after I-394. Continue south along the western edge of Cedar Lake.

18.5   Turn left onto Dean Boulevard to connect to the Lake of the Isles for an approximate 3-mile loop before returning back to this point. When you return to this point, turn left (south) to continue onto Dean Parkway (which will quickly change name to Calhoun Parkway) along the western edge of Lake Calhoun

23.8   Turn right (south) onto the Lake Harriet Bike Trail.

25.0   Turn right (southwest) to cycle along the western edge of Lake Harriet.

26.8   Turn right (southeast) away from Lake Harriet and onto W. Minnehaha Parkway.

31.0   Turn left (north) onto a bike trail that will turn east over Minnehaha Creek. Continue on this path for about a mile until hitting Hiawatha Avenue.

32.0   Turn right (southeast) onto a bike path alongside Hiawatha Avenue. Stay on the path as it runs into Minnehaha Parkway and follow it east around a traffic circle. Continue cycling east on this path as it follows Godfrey Parkway and bends north along W. River Parkway at the Mississippi River.

33.0   Follow W. River Parkway the final 7 miles back to the start at the southern end of the Stone Arch Bridge.

40.0   Finish at the Stone Arch Bridge.

Ride Information

Local Events and Attractions: Minneapolis–Saint Paul International Film Festival; mspfilm .org/festivals/mspiff/

Northern Spark; arts festival; June; northernspark.org

Stone Arch Bridge Festival; weekend of art and music; June; stonearchbridgefestival .com

21 Minnesota River Bluffs to Lake Minnetonka Loop Ramble

This nearly 30-mile loop connects two of the region's most popular rail trails that give cyclists a taste of aggregate trail instead of the paved paths that are more common around the Twin Cities. In all, it's an easy-to-navigate ride through the southwestern suburbs and exurbs of Minneapolis with no shortage of scenery to make the miles fly by.

Start: Depot Coffee House, 9451 Excelsior Blvd., Hopkins

Distance: 27.5-mile loop

Riding time: About 2 hours

Terrain and trail surface: Aggregate trail with some road cycling

Traffic and hazards: These trails are open only to human power and are used mostly by training and recreational cyclists. However, walkers and runners also use the trail, and it is best to be courteous and give them the right of way when encountered.

Things to see: Depot Coffee House, Lake Minnetonka

Getting there: From I-394 W, take US 169 S toward CR 3/Excelsior Boulevard in Hopkins. Take the Excelsior Boulevard/CR 3 exit and turn left onto Excelsior Boulevard. The Depot Coffee House will be on the right.

The Ride

Perhaps it's the cyclist stereotype in me (or new urban millennial stereotype), but I love a good coffee shop. Something about the smell of fresh java, the sounds of those science-class instruments going to work at the hands of a capable barista, and a good coffee shop's general community feel leaves a smile on my face. Now mix all of that with a cycling focus, and I'm sold.

That's Depot Coffee House in Hopkins. Anchored right on the Minnesota River Bluffs LRT Regional Trail with the Cedar Lake LRT Regional Trail across the street on Excelsior Boulevard, the Depot Coffee House makes for a perfect cycling gathering point. Inside they sell anything you need for a pre-ride boost or even something small, like a Clif Bar, to take along for the ride. Outside they have some basic maintenance equipment should you need to pump up your tires a bit or raise or lower a seat. The Depot Coffee House in and of itself is a big selling

Slightly thicker tires are required out here west of the Twin Cities. JOE BAUR

point for giving this ride its own chapter. The other selling point, of course, is the Minnesota River Bluffs LRT Regional Trail.

It doesn't take long for this paved path to turn into aggregate trail, so make sure you've got tires that won't disappoint you halfway into the ride. There's no deviation from the trail for about 10 miles, when you'll turn off onto Pioneer Trail, which, despite its name, is actually a road. You're on this road for less than 2 miles, but there is a path on the northern side of the road if you don't feel like mixing it up with cars. From there it's a right onto Powers Boulevard, which will get you into Excelsior in a little under 6 miles. Now, perhaps I'm a bit unobservant at times, but I found it easy to lose track of where the Lake Minnetonka LRT Regional Trail picks up in Excelsior. My Strava recording, showing a squiggly red

THE DEPOT

In case the name didn't give it away, the Depot Coffee House is constructed within a renovated train depot in Hopkins, Minnesota. Besides serving java and delicious little goodies, it's a youth community project and (obviously) a trailhead area for bikes. Local students worked together with regional supporters in 1998 to open the Depot as a chemical-free environment for teens.

Minnesota River Bluffs to Lake Minnetonka Loop Ramble

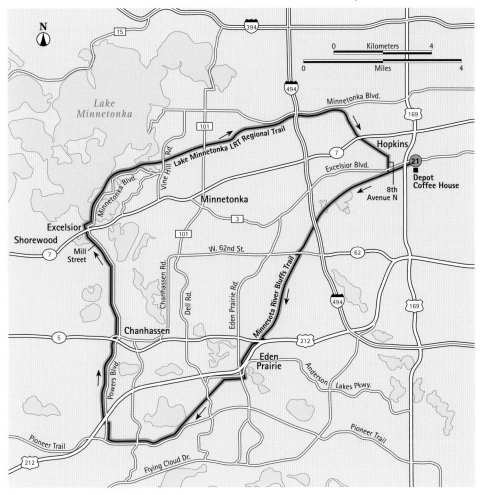

line circling Minnetonka Boulevard, attests to that very fact. Just know if you see a McDonald's on your right, you've gone too far. You want to stay along Minnetonka Boulevard, on the western side, as it shoots north seemingly into the lake. Fear not, I'm confident you'll spot the trail better than I did.

This should all be relatively familiar if you've already done the Dakota to Minnetonka Loop Ramble, except instead of turning off onto Tonkawood, you'll continue straight through to Minnetonka Mills until the trail comes to an end in downtown Hopkins at 8th Avenue N. Then it's a straight shot south until you hit the already familiar Minnesota River Bluffs LRT Regional Trail, hanging a left to head back to the Depot Coffee House, where you started.

Miles and Directions

0.0   Start on the Minnesota River Bluffs LRT Regional Trail from Depot Coffee House, cycling west for 10 miles.

10.0   Turn right (west) onto Pioneer Trail for about 2 miles to Powers Boulevard.

12.0   Turn right (north) onto Powers Boulevard and follow it 6 miles into the town of Excelsior. Note that the name of the road will change to Mill Street just before Excelsior.

18.0   Turn right onto Excelsior Boulevard and look for the Lake Minnetonka LRT Regional Trail on your left (north) in about 0.2 mile.

18.2   Turn left onto the Lake Minnetonka LRT Regional Trail, following it without deviation for just under 10 miles.

27.5   Reach the end of the Lake Minnetonka LRT Regional Trail in downtown Hopkins. Turn right onto 8th Avenue N and follow it for about 0.3 mile until you rejoin the Minnesota River Bluffs LRT Regional Trail. Turn left back onto the trail and arrive back at Depot Coffee House.

22 Saint Paul Grand Round Cruise

A beautiful 30(ish)-mile loop around Saint Paul that gives cyclists a taste of everything it has to offer, from scenic green parkways to residential and urban riding. This route can also easily connect to a number of other rides in the book for additional miles.

Start: At the Civil War Monument in Shadow Falls Park Preserve off Mississippi River Boulevard and Summit Avenue

Distance: 28.6–mile loop

Riding time: About 2 hours

Terrain and trail surface: Paved path and road, mostly flat

Traffic and hazards: There will be a mixture of trail and vehicular traffic depending on when you opt for roads or separated bike paths. A substantial portion of the ride travels on painted bike lanes alongside vehicular traffic.

Things to see: Saint Paul, Lake Phalen, Lake Como, Mississippi River

Getting there: From I-94, get off at Cretin Avenue S toward Mississippi River Boulevard. Turn right and take a quick left onto Mississippi River Boulevard alongside Shadow Falls Park Preserve. The Civil War Monument and a parking lot will be on your right in about 0.3 mile. GPS: N44°56.49387' / W93°11.91043'

The Ride

Being two formidable cities in such close proximity, there's naturally a bit of a sibling rivalry between Minneapolis and Saint Paul. Rightly (say the Minneapolitans) or unfairly (say those from Saint Paul), the latter city often gets the short end of the stick in national conversations. Minneapolitans like to point out that all of the professional sports teams called Minneapolis home until the Minnesota Wild came in as an expansion team. Even then some locals phrased it as if they were throwing Saint Paul a bone. Folks from Saint Paul will say they don't care, some Minneapolitans will say, "Yeah, you do!" poking them endlessly like a good sibling does.

Saint Paul also gets left out of national and international conversations when it comes to talk about cycling. It's usually Minneapolis that makes the top of the list, not Saint Paul. If Saint Paul gets mentioned, it's usually as an aside when talking about how great Minneapolis is.

Pedaling away from the start of the Saint Paul Grand Round JOE BAUR

I will definitely say that it is, indeed, unfair. Locals and visitors alike can, and will, debate which is the better cycling city. For me, I say you're right wherever you land, because both are far beyond where the rest of the United States currently resides. As far as Saint Paul is concerned, cycling around the city on the approximately 30-mile Saint Paul Grand Round is a treat any cyclist will love with its mixture of parkways surrounded by green space and city riding. It's not here merely for balance between the Twin Cities, but because it really is one of the best rides you can get on two wheels in the region. Even better, it fits right in with the connectivity of the region. Linking this ride with the Cedar Lake to Midtown and Hiawatha Ramble or the Minneapolis Grand Round Cruise is a cinch using the Lake Street–Marshall Bridge. Or you can throw in Gateway to Brown's Creek State Trail, Stillwater Ramble on the northern end of this cruise, as I did when recording the two respective rides. It bears repeating that such connectivity is rare whether you're looking at the United States or the world as a whole, and Saint Paul is an essential ingredient in making it all work.

My gushing aside, let's look at just the Saint Paul Grand Round. As a loop, there are a number of potential starting points. I opted for the Civil War Monument at S. Mississippi River Boulevard and Summit Avenue for its proximity to Minneapolis, should you wish to connect it with other rides. And it's a scenic corner in its own right.

From here I pedaled south through Mississippi Gorge Regional Park for a lovely parkway ride not entirely unlike what you'll get on the other side of the river along River Parkway in the Minneapolis Grand Ground Cruise. You'll follow along on marked, separated bike lanes for most of the initial route as it wraps around the city of Saint Paul. Comfortable road riders can just as easily hop on the road if the paths are busy, but there are sections later on where you'll want to be on the path rather than mix with the high-speed traffic. About 4 miles in, you can leave Shepard Road and duck into Hidden Falls and Crosby Farm Parks. There are routes within the parks you can glide across and still get back up to Shepard Road on the other end. For the sake of the book, I continued along Shepard without the deviation.

Once on Johnson, you'll be taking painted bike lanes almost exclusively for the remainder of the ride. Some paths will pop up as you approach Lake Phalen—a loop you're welcome to add for additional miles—but it's true road riding from here on out as you follow Johnson onto Wheelock Parkway.

At about 18 miles, around I-35E, you'll hit the Gateway Trail. (*Option:* Carefully pull over onto the northern grass and follow a footpath up to the trail should you wish to add that ride to the Saint Paul Grand Round.) Otherwise, you simply continue west on Wheelock toward Como Lake—another loop you're welcome to add for additional miles. (*Option:* To trim about 1.5 miles, you can skate south around the lake onto Como Avenue to continue west.)

Como will get you over to Raymond Avenue, which skirts you through more residential areas that become progressively more urban. This also takes you through, at least at the time of riding, some of the shoddier roads on this ride with a number of potholes and cracks plaguing the thoroughfare. But it doesn't last long as you pedal past University to get over to Pelham Boulevard, which sends you due south to the familiar Mississippi River Boulevard for the last mile of the ride back to the Civil War Monument.

Miles and Directions

0.0 Start at the Civil War Monument near the intersection of Mississippi River Boulevard and Summit Avenue. Pedal south primarily on a separated bike path along Mississippi River Boulevard as it wraps east around the city.

Saint Paul Grand Round Cruise

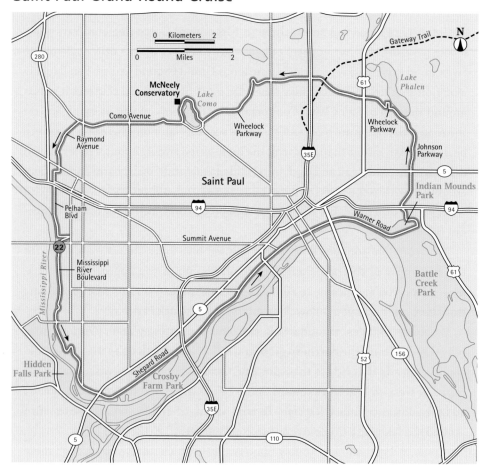

4.0 Reach the junction for Hidden Falls and Crosby Farm Parks. Don't go downhill to continue along Shepard Road—stay to the left (north).

10.8 Shepard Road becomes Warner Road just east of downtown Saint Paul.

12.4 Turn left (north) onto a bike path toward Burns Avenue.

12.6 Turn left (west) onto Burns Avenue followed by a quick right (north) onto the painted bike lanes of Johnson Parkway.

15.1 The Johnson Parkway intersects with E. Shore Drive. Continue west, south of Lake Phalen, and the road becomes Wheelock Parkway.

17.4 Wheelock Parkway passes the Gateway Trail.

21.6 Arrive at Como Lake. Turn right (west) to do about 1.5 miles around the northern end of the lake. Follow the bike path around the lake until you reach Como Avenue.

23.1 Turn right (west) onto Como Avenue.

25.4 Turn left (southeast) onto Raymond Avenue.

26.6 Pass University Avenue and turn right (west) onto Myrtle Avenue. In about 0.1 mile, turn left (south) onto Pelham Boulevard.

27.6 Rejoin with Mississippi River Boulevard and continue cycling south. Follow it for the last mile, back to the Civil War Monument.

28.6 Return to the Civil War Monument where you started.

23 Gateway to Brown's Creek State Trail, Stillwater Ramble

This relaxing trip is as straightforward as it gets: The entire ride is on paved paths—without road crossings—to Pine Point Regional Park on the Gateway State Trail and then over to Stillwater, Minnesota, on the Brown's Creek State Trail.

Start: Where the Gateway State Trail meets Wheelock Parkway

Distance: 46-mile out and back

Riding time: About 3 hours

Terrain and trail surface: Paved and mostly flat

Traffic and hazards: These trails are open only to human power and are used mostly by training and commuting cyclists. However, walkers and runners also use the trail, and it is best to be courteous and give them the right of way when encountered.

Things to see: Pine Point Regional Park, Stillwater

Getting there: Take Edgerton Street north to Wheelock Parkway. Turn left onto Wheelock Parkway; the Gateway Trail intersects in less than 0.5 mile on your right. GPS: N44°59.38422' / W93°04.97007'

The Ride

The Saint Paul trailhead has been under construction for quite some time. Without construction, the Gateway State Trail starts a little farther south from Wheelock Parkway off L'Orient Street by Maryland Avenue and Trout Book Nature Sanctuary. Perhaps construction will be completed by the time this book is released. Your best bet is to consult the Minnesota Department of Natural Resources (dnr.state.mn.us) for up-to-date information.

When it came to deciding where to start this trail for the book, I looked at what connected best with other rides in the book. Wheelock Parkway just so happens to be a main thoroughfare in the Saint Paul Grand Round Cruise, so I decided to hop on the Gateway State Trail right off Wheelock Parkway.

You'll know you've arrived when you see the Gateway State Trail bridge hanging over Wheelock Parkway. From Wheelock Parkway, you'll have to dismount your bike and take it onto the grass and follow a footpath up to the trail. It's not as inconspicuous as it sounds. In fact, I discovered the little footpath by following others doing the same. Just use caution in slowing down on Wheelock and make sure any other cyclists or vehicular traffic behind you is aware that you're slowing down and stopping.

Once you get up to the Gateway Trail, it's smooth sailing for the rest of the ride on another one of those densely wooded trails that feels completely removed from urban Saint Paul. (That could also be because you're actively pedaling away from the city.) It's about 16.5 miles to the end of the Gateway Trail in Pine Point Regional Park if you take it as a straight shot. At 12 miles in, you'll come to a junction for Brown's Creek State Trail that takes you 6 miles east over to the small city of Stillwater, Minnesota, on the Saint Croix River, with Wisconsin on the other side.

This of course means you have options to shorten or extend your ride, like any other road ride in this book. If you're not up for the miles, I can admit that there's nothing remarkable that you'd be missing by pedaling the extra 4 (8 round-trip) miles to Pine Point Regional Park from the Brown's Creek State Trail junction. It's also worth noting that the Gateway Trail simply ends when it runs into Norell Avenue N. If you do make it up to Pine Point Park and want to make a pit stop (i.e., pee), there's a footpath on the northern edge of the bike trail just before you

A consistent, leafy, and paved view along the Gateway State Trail north of Saint Paul JOE BAUR

STILLWATER

Stillwater, Minnesota, is a lovely small city of about 18,000 people. Considering its position right off the Brown's Creek State Trail, it makes a great option for any cyclists looking to split the ride up with an overnight stay.

Its settlement dates back to treaties signed between the United States government and local Ojibwa and Dakota Nations that permitted settlement in the Saint Croix Valley in 1837. Stillwater, named after the calm waters of the Saint Croix, is still considered by many to be the birthplace of Minnesota. Taking into account its historic importance, it became a finalist for erecting an important public institution for the young territory of Minnesota. Minneapolis was awarded with the University of Minnesota, Saint Paul received capital honors, and Stillwater got—hold onto your hats—the territory's first prison. That's right, the Minnesota Territorial Prison opened in 1853 in Stillwater.

It seems a bit like a backhanded compliment in retrospect, but visiting today's Stillwater by bike more than makes up for it.

hit the road. That footpath will get you up to the parking lot and restroom area, where you can take a break and refill your water bottles.

Brown's Creek State Trail drops you off right into the heart of Stillwater's riverfront. I'll admit I was a bit disappointed by the amount of space devoted to car parking. In fact, the last little jaunt on Brown's Creek State Trail (once you get out of the woods) cuts through football fields of parking space. That said, the adjacent North Lowell Park proved to be an inviting green space with large crowds out enjoying the summer weekend along the Saint Croix River.

After enjoying the riverfront, you can simply backtrack to where you started on the Gateway Trail and either continue with the Saint Paul Grand Round or head home.

Miles and Directions

0.0   Start on the Gateway Trail off of Wheelock Parkway and pedal northeast for 12 miles.

Gateway to Brown's Creek State Trail, Stillwater Ramble

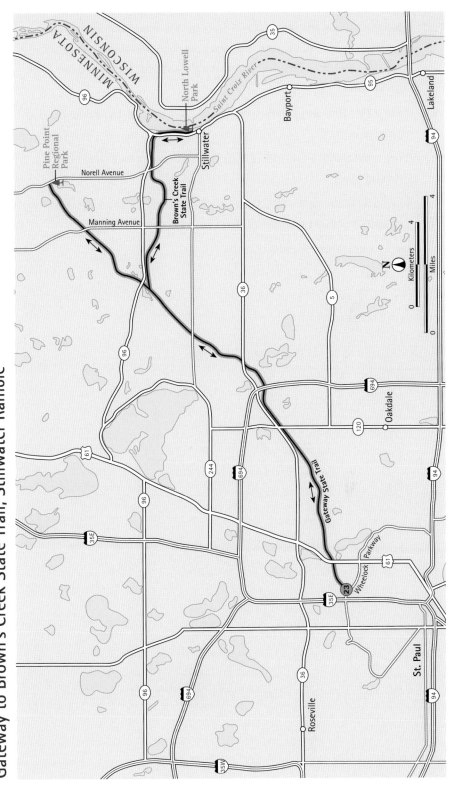

12.0 Reach the Gateway and Brown's Creek State Trails junction. Turn right for Brown's Creek if you want to shave some miles and head right to Stillwater, Minnesota. Otherwise, stay left to continue heading straight and northeast toward Pine Point Regional Park.

16.6 Arrive at Pine Point Regional Park. When ready, turn back for 4.6 miles to the aforementioned junction.

21.3 Turn left (east) onto Brown's Creek State Trail and follow it for 6 miles into Stillwater.

27.5 Arrive in Stillwater, on the Saint Croix River. When ready, backtrack to the Gateway Trail junction and take that back to where you started.

46.0 Arrive back at Wheelock Parkway.

24 Medicine Lake to Elm Creek Ramble

Here is yet another scenic ride with no shortage of lakeside views as you ramble alongside Medicine Lake and up to Elm Creek Park Reserve, arguably one of the region's most impressive parks with approximately 15 miles of cycling paths to enjoy.

Start: At the Medicine Lake Regional Trail trailhead at the southern edge of Medicine Lake and off the Luce Line Regional Trail

Distance: 45.7-mile lollipop

Riding time: About 3 hours

Terrain and trail surface: Paved and mostly flat

Traffic and hazards: These trails are open only to human power and are used mostly by training and commuting cyclists. However, walkers and runners also use the trail, and it is best to be courteous and give them the right of way when encountered.

Things to see: Medicine Lake, French Regional Park, Fish Lake Regional Park, Elm Creek Park Reserve

Getting there: From MN 55, drive west to US 169 N. Stay on US 169 for only 0.3 mile, when you'll exit to Plymouth Avenue N. Turn left onto Plymouth Avenue N, followed by a quick right on the other side of the highway onto Kilmer Lane N. Follow Kilmer Lane N briefly until 17th Avenue N. This will run right into a parking lot along the Medicine Lake Regional Trail and Medicine Lake. GPS: N44°59.69105' / W93°24.46865'

The Ride

Twin Cities weather can be tricky. In my experience, weather forecasts tend to err on the side of gloom and doom. I've canceled a number of rides due to stormy forecasts that turned out to be gorgeous sunny days. So when I woke up the morning of this Medicine Lake ride and saw a 30 to 50 percent chance of storms in the midafternoon, I shrugged it off and started pedaling from Whittier over to Medicine Lake.

From the start of the Medicine Lake Regional Trail on the southern edge of Medicine Lake, it's easy to see why early vacationers would spend their holidays here and just as easy to see why today's quieter souls settle here. Like everything else in Twin Cities cycling, following along the Medicine Lake Regional Trail is no challenging feat, even when you inevitably zone out as you admire the scenery

Near the trailhead alongside Medicine Lake with threatening clouds overhead JOE BAUR

of Medicine Lake and its adjacent French Regional Park. Things do take a rather ugly exurban turn north of French Regional Park as you pedal alongside high speed roads. It's always nice to have the bike paths, but I don't think anyone truly enjoys riding with 40- to 50-mile-per-hour traffic whizzing by.

There happened to be a bit of construction when I rode, taking me on a bit of a detour 5 miles in. (The Miles and Directions below reflect what the route is *supposed* to be.) While the bike path continues, it kicked me off the Medicine Lake Regional Trail longer than I would've liked as I meandered alongside Northwest Boulevard into Maple Grove. Using my trusty Google Map, I managed to finagle my way back to the route once I realized those orange detour signs had disappeared and left me to my own devices. Once I was able to rejoin the proper trail of Bass Lake Road, I was treated to a beautiful and winding tree-lined route through Fish Lake Regional Park and up the rest of the way to Elm Creek Park Reserve.

As I neared Elm Creek, I started noticing some ominous clouds approaching. Sure enough, when I hopped off at the Elm Creek junction for a snack, my phone alerted me to imminent thunderstorms. Rather than turn tail and run, I kept those loyal FalconGuide readers in mind as I braved the incoming threat to finish my lollipop loop around Elm Creek Park Reserve.

Unfortunately my bravery only lasted until the storm inevitably caught up with me.

"Guess we're getting rained on after all!" more than one cyclist said to me in passing, with that notable Minnesotan cheer. Before I got even halfway through the loop, the pounding rain came before I could plan a reasonable escape.

So, with my precious electronics in mind, I did cut the loop short at only 7 miles instead of my planned 10. But keep in mind you also have Elm Creek hike and mountain bike chapters in this book. Methinks I haven't exactly short-changed this lovely slice of green space. Besides, the route I ended up taking was as scenic as anything else I would've experienced.

At least, that's what I gathered in between the raindrops.

With the storm picking up steam, I paused in tunnels to check out the forecast. Looked like this one was going to be around for a while. So rather than get cold and tighten up, I plunged ahead on the Medicine Lake Regional Trail. However, this time, when I returned to that pesky detour, I opted to skirt around ole Johnny Law and found my way to this alleged construction that forced me several miles off the trail. Turned out all I had to do to avoid the construction was hop off my bike for not even a 100-foot walk—much better than another 5 miles in pouring rain. Luckily this construction will no doubt be finished by the time this book goes out, and you won't have to suffer through the same detour to stay on the much more worthy Medicine Lake Regional Trail.

The rain had settled to merely an inconvenient thump by the time I returned to French Regional Park. It was just inconvenient enough that I missed my left turn to stay on the Medicine Lake Regional Trail and did a mile loop around the park—because I guess I wasn't wet enough already. But as I pedaled over a couple of lovely wooden bridges within this short loop, the creeks lined with playful-looking green lily pads, I thought to myself, "Okay, this is book worthy."

Medicine Lake to Elm Creek Ramble

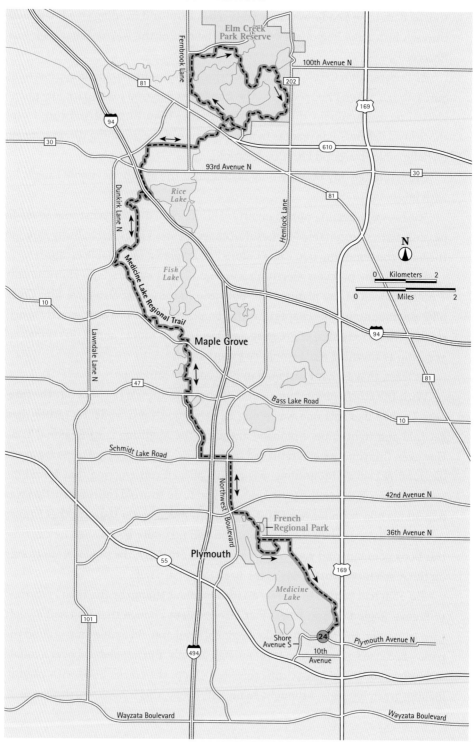

From there it was just another short 3 miles back to the Medicine Lake Regional Trailhead to finish the ride.

Miles and Directions

0.0 Start at the Medicine Lake Regional Trail junction off the Luce Line Regional Trail. Follow this trail alongside Medicine Lake and through French Regional Park.

2.8 Arrive at French Regional Park and continue pedaling northwest along the trail.

8.4 Enter Fish Lake Regional Park, cycling through on the Medicine Lake Regional Trail. Continue along the winding path for another 10.3 miles until Elm Creek Park Reserve.

18.7 Arrive at the Elm Creek Park Reserve junction and turn left (west). Stay on the outside path for about 3 miles.

21.6 Stay straight, cycling east toward Pineview Lane. Turn right (south) onto Pineview Lane and continue following the trail between Mud Lake and Goose Lake.

26.1 Arrive at James Deane Parkway and follow the trail south as it travels alongside and across the road. Continue here for another 2 miles until you return to the Elm Creek Park Reserve junction where you began the loop, then backtrack on the Medicine Lake Regional Trail to the start.

42.7 Return to French Regional Park and take the 1-mile loop around the park by turning right off Medicine Lake Trail.

43.7 Back at Medicine Lake Trail, follow it south to the trailhead.

45.7 Reach the trailhead and the finish.

MOUNTAIN BIKING

It's not uncommon for cyclists to dabble between road and mountain biking. Thanks to a number of trail options and the Minnesota Off-Road Cyclists (MORC), a nonprofit committed to maintaining and growing the system, the Twin Cities are just as good for mountain biking as they are celebrated for road cycling. These trails are typically open from April through November with closures taking place for maintenance or following wet weather. The freeze/thaw period is another season to keep off the trails between fall and spring. Luckily you can always refer to MORC at morcmtb.org for up-to-date information on trail closures; passionate riders and volunteers post through all hours of the night to catch eager riders hoping to hit the trails first thing in the morning.

Porter whizzes through the obstacle course at Carver Lake. JOE BAUR

Oh, and did you think Minnesotans stop cycling in the winter? Wrong. Fat tire riders can take their bikes on the trails so long as conditions are not wet or muddy.

BIKE SHOPS

Minneapolis

Angry Catfish Bicycle + Coffee Bar: 4208 S. 28th Ave., Minneapolis 55406; (612) 722-1538; angrycatfishbicycle.com

Charlie's Tangletown Bike Shop: 322 W. 48th St., Minneapolis 55409; (612) 259-8180; tangletownbikeshop.com

Erik's: 2800 Lyndale Ave. S, Ste. 1, Minneapolis 55408; 612-872-8600; www.eriksbikeshop.com

Flanders Brothers Cycle: 2707 Lyndale Ave. S, Minneapolis 55408; (612) 872-6994; flandersbros.com

Freewheel Bike Midtown Bike Center: 2834 10th Ave. S, Minneapolis 55407; (612) 238-4447; freewheelbikecenter.com

The Hub Bike Co-op: 3020 Minnehaha Ave., Minneapolis 55406; (612) 729-0437; thehubbikecoop.org

One On One Bicycle Studio: 117 N. Washington Ave., Minneapolis 55401; (612) 371-9565; oneononebike.com

Penn Cycle: 710 W. Lake St., Minneapolis 55408; (612) 822-2228; penncycle.com

Perennial Cycle: 3342 Hennepin Ave. S, Minneapolis 55408; (612) 827-8000; perennialcycle.com

Sunrise Cyclery: 2901 Blaisdell Ave. S, Minneapolis 55408; (612) 824-6144; sunrisecyclerympls.com

Two Wheels Bike Shop: 1014 W. 27th St., Minneapolis 55408; (612) 735-7345

Venture North Bikes: 1830 Glenwood Ave., Minneapolis 55405; (612) 377-3029; venturenorthbwc.org

Saint Paul

Capital Deals: 710 Smith Ave. S, Saint Paul 55107; (651) 222-8380; capitaldealsonline.com

Cycles for Change: 712 University Ave. W, Saint Paul 55104; (651) 222-2080; cyclesforchange.org

Express Bike Shop: 1158 Selby Ave., Saint Paul 55104; (651) 644-9660; exbike .com

Grand Performance: 1938 Grand Ave., Saint Paul 55105; (651) 699-2640; gp bicycles.com

Lowertown Bike Shop: 214 E. 4th St., #160, Saint Paul 55101; (651) 222-0775; lowertownbikeshop.com

Now Bikes & Fitness: 75 N. Snelling Ave., Saint Paul 55104; (651) 644-2534; nowbikes-fitness.com

Seven Spokes: 1044 Cleveland Ave. S, Saint Paul 55116; (651) 698-2453; seven spokesbikeshop.com

25 Carver Lake Park

A creation of the Minnesota Off-Road Cyclists (MORC), this 4-mile loop rolls over a majority of the park's 5.5 miles of trail. Enjoy the views of Carver Lake as you cruise along before diving into the wooded interior along the main trail. This is a great loop for intermediate riders. Experienced riders can do a few laps for practice and play around on the multi-lap training ground full of obstacles.

Start: Carver Lake Park, 3175 Century Ave. S in Woodbury

Distance: 4-mile loop

Riding time: 30 to 45 minutes

Terrain and surface type: Rolling trail with occasional flat sections

Highlights: Excellent views of Carver Lake along the ride

Hazards: Some exposed roots and logs

Maps: *DeLorme: Minnesota Atlas & Gazetteer* map 71; city of Woodbury map at ci.woodbury.mn.us

Getting there: From I-494 and Lake Road, follow Lake Road east 0.3 mile to Courtly Road. Turn right and head west 0.5 mile to Century Avenue. Turn left to the park entrance on the south side of Carver Lake. Follow the road to the western end of the parking lot. GPS: N44 54.237' / W92 58.789'

The Ride

This 4-mile loop is an easy pick for Twin Cities riders, especially those who call Saint Paul home. It's not uncommon for some cyclists to ride to the park itself before taking on the loop.

I, however, arrived with Porter Million—a former racer with Larson Cycle Racing and current "Dirt Boss" for MORC after finishing four years on its board of directors. Being far more the professional out of our pair, Porter led the way, while I followed closely behind on my rental from Angry Catfish in Minneapolis.

Indeed, the trail at Carver Lake Park is a highlight of MORC's work and of the mountain-biking options within the great Twin Cities area. Excellent views of Carver Lake come early on the ride as you continue cruising along the rolling hillside. There's a relaxing flow to a nice portion of the ride. Sharp turns are aplenty here as well, which is why the trail map looks like a plate of spaghetti or an aerial of a city built before grids.

A peek at the mountain biker's playground at Carver Lake JOE BAUR

You'll also find flat sections of the park with wide-open views of the sky above and trail connectors for those who want to repeat certain loops within the trail. Others will take on the entire loop multiple times, but Porter and I were content completing just the one loop, considering we had another ride on our agenda for the day.

Near the end of the ride, there's a bit of an obstacle course or playground for expert riders, including a balance beam and boardwalk to ride over. This is where those with a substantial amount of riding experience and miles under their respective belts like to hone or tune those mountain-biking skills that make novices stare, dumbfounded.

After playing around (or skipping it to avoid injury), a modest climb returns you to a paved path through white pine and back around the archery range. Continue following the path west before it hairpins back and forth a couple more times, leading right back to the park entrance.

Miles and Directions

0.0 Start at the trailhead, head west.

0.2 Ride the balance beam and bridge to the first turn.

Carver Lake Park

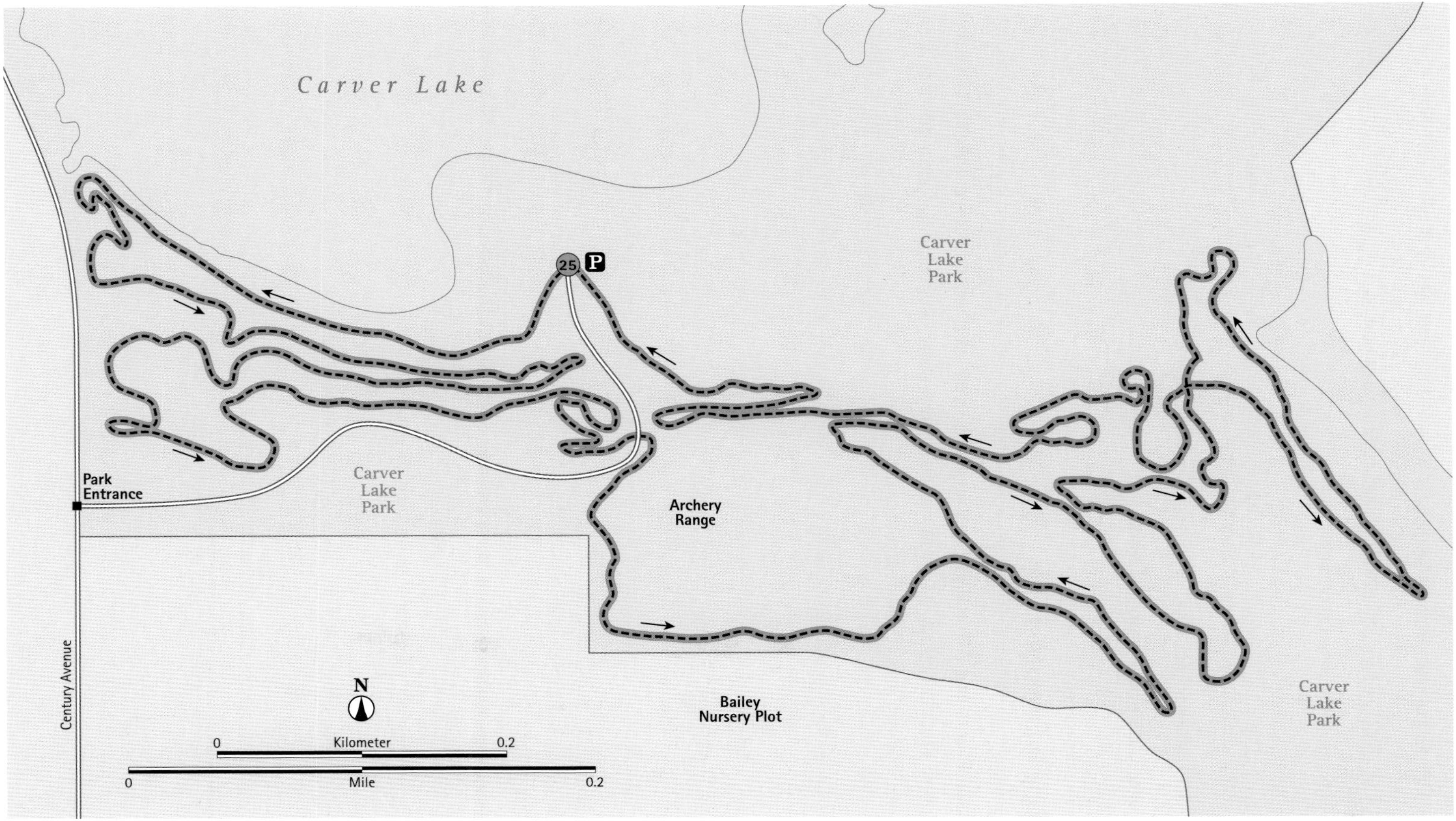

Carver Lake

Carver Lake Park

Carver Lake Park

Carver Lake Park

Archery Range

Bailey Nursery Plot

Park Entrance

Century Avenue

25

P

N

Kilometer

Mile

0   0.2

0   0.2

0.3	Follow the turn as it heads back east.
1.0	Ride over the boardwalk bridge, crossing a ravine.
1.5	Pass by the archery range.
2.4	Approach a junction with a paved path, cycling straight across.
2.9	Cross the paved path a second time.
3.7	Make a final turn northwesterly toward the exit.
4.0	Arrive back at the trailhead.

Ride Information

Local Events and Attractions: Ojibway Park, north-northeast of Carver Lake Park, hosts the annual Woodbury Days, a two-day town festival in late August with sporting events, a carnival, and live music; woodburydays.com.

26 Theodore Wirth Park

Theodore Wirth Park is not only steeped in local history, it is also packed corner to corner with year-round activities for all outdoor lovers, be it on the golf course (club or disc), hiking trails, swimming beach, or skis. This short but lively fat tire trip through the woods is a gem in the Minneapolis park system, with an orbit of feeder trails for express access and après-ride distractions.

Start: Trailhead on Glenwood Avenue, southeast of Wirth Lake

Distance: 4.5-mile double loop

Riding time: 30 to 40 minutes

Terrain and surface type: Rolling hills on packed singletrack, with short sections of cross-country ski trails

Highlights: Said obstacles above, along with fast and flowing trails in scenic woods, switchback climbs, jumps

Hazards: Rock gardens and other obstacles, hikers, light traffic at road crossings

Maps: *DeLorme: Minnesota Atlas & Gazetteer* map 70; maps through minneapolis parks.org

Getting there: From I-394, exit at Penn Avenue and head north to Glenwood Avenue, then right toward the east to the parking area at the south end of Wirth Lake. The south loop starts at the northwest corner of MN 55 and Theodore Wirth Parkway. GPS: N44° 58.905' / W93° 19.248'

To reach the north loop, ride west on Glenwood Avenue and turn right (north) onto the paved bike trail that runs along Theodore Wirth Parkway, past the railroad tracks, to the Luce Line Regional Trail. Follow the Luce Line to the mountain bike trail gate. GPS: N44° 98.866' / W93° 33.121'

The Ride

T-Wirth is like a Tootsie Roll Pop. Ask a Twin Cities mountain biker to describe Theodore Wirth Park, and a likely answer resembles the iconic lollipop, with a shiny, enticing exterior and a bonus treat in the middle. This stellar trail system is the result of a solid relationship between MORC, the Minneapolis Park & Recreation Board, and Minneapolis Off-Road Cycling Advocates (MOCA). Initially just a city demonstration project, the T-Wirth trails show off a sustainably built, safe, and just plain fun trail that is compatible with the park's natural landscapes. The fast and flowing trail rolls around in the park's old hardwood forest

Serpentine turn on the trail NICK PETTIS

on a masterfully planned route perfect for intermediate riders, and scattered obstacles like log piles and jumps challenge experienced riders. Development of more trail miles is in the works, including more challenging terrain and technical features.

What's especially cool about the Wirth trails is the spiderweb of bike trails leading to the park from all around the city, like the Cedar Lake LRT Regional and Luce Line Regional Trails. It's a great warm-up and fun to cruise post-ride to your favorite watering hole.

Start the short, under-1-mile south lollipop on the singletrack past the trail kiosk and veer left at the first split, climbing gradually to the twisty Enchanted Forest section. All of T-Wirth's main trails run clockwise and one-way, so just follow the path. At the top end of Enchanted Forest, you can roll onto the paved trail to reach the north loop, or continue south on Skyline back to the trailhead.

For the longer north loop, follow the paved trail north over the railroad track to the Luce Line Regional Trail, take a left along the south side of the golf course, and head west to the mountain bike trail gate. The path starts with mostly easy-going curves on the Conundrum and Snake Trails paralleling the railroad track, with a challenging uphill rock garden, then winds deeper into the woods on

Theodore Wirth Park—South Loop

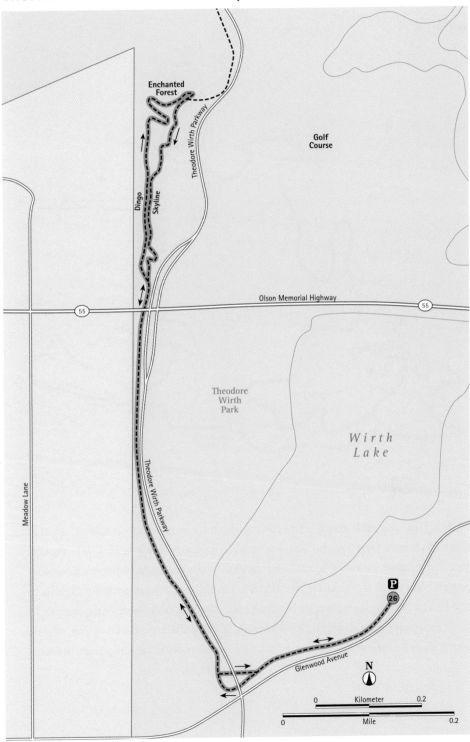

Enchanted
Forest

Dingo

Skyline

Theodore Wirth Parkway

Golf
Course

Olson Memorial Highway

55

55

Meadow Lane

Theodore
Wirth
Park

Theodore Wirth Parkway

*Wirth
Lake*

P
26

Glenwood Avenue

N

| 0 | Kilometer | 0.2 |
| 0 | Mile | 0.2 |

Theodore Wirth Park—North Loop

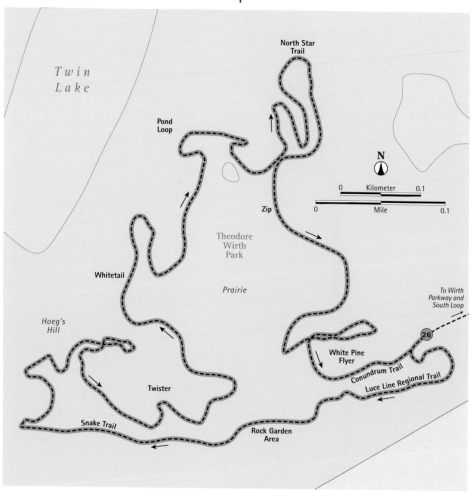

Hoeg's Hill. The trail crosses the hiking/ski trail on several occasions, so stay alert for hikers. The Twister section stays true to its name and winds around in a convoluted series of bends and rollers to the west side of the oak-dotted prairie. North of the prairie, the Pond Loop follows a hammerhead course to the North Star Trail and a spur heading into adjacent neighborhoods. Stay right here, starting your return trip southbound. Cruise the long curve of Zip, and fly along sloped turns and a winding downhill, with an optional jump near the exit.

Miles and Directions

0.0 Start at the Glenwood Avenue trailhead.

0.4 Reach the top of the Enchanted Forest trail and access to paved bike path. Stay right to finish loop.

0.7 Return to trailhead. Follow the paved trail north across the railroad tracks.

1.1 Arrive at the junction with Luce Line Regional Trail. Turn left into the woods.

1.2 Turn left off the Luce Line onto the singletrack trail into the woods.

1.4 Start climbing toward the rock garden.

1.9 Arrive at the Hoeg's Hill section.

2.6 Dive into the Twister stretch, and curve around to edge of the prairie.

4.1 Start the hammerhead loop around the pond.

4.3 Veer right at the junction with the spur trail to adjacent neighborhoods.

4.5 Return back to the Luce Line Regional Trail. Retrace this and the paved path back to the Glenwood Avenue trailhead.

Ride Information

Restaurants: Summertime, patio table, and Sebastian Joe's waffle cone—three ingredients for a perfect day. Go here after your ride to unwind and reload. Less than 2 miles from T-Wirth on the bike trails. 1007 W. Franklin Ave., Minneapolis; (612) 870-0065; sebastian joesicecream.com

Local Events and Attractions: The city of Lakes Loppet cross-country skiing festival in early February livens up winter with a host of ski races, tours, skijoring competitions, and a bike race held on a frozen course near Uptown; cityoflakesloppet.com.

South Minneapolis sets the stage for family fun and blazing-fast racing at the mid-summer Southside Sprint, with kids' races, stunt shows, great grub, and go-fast pro events. In the south side's 48th and Chicago neighborhood; southsidesprint.com.

—Steve Johnson

27 Murphy-Hanrehan Park Reserve

A local favorite for over twenty years, the trail system at Murphy has risen to the highest ranks of fat tire destinations, thanks to the dedication and cooperation of the Three Rivers Park District and Minnesota Off-Road Cyclists (MORC). Explore three expertly designed loops in this undeveloped, wildlife-packed park reserve.

Start: Trailhead at 15501 Murphy Lake Rd., Savage

Distance: 3.5 miles

Riding time: About 45 minutes

Terrain and surface type: Rolling, with a few punchy climbs, on sublime singletrack trail through open meadows and dense forest

Highlights: Vibrant avian life and ground-based wildlife like beavers, deer, fox, and muskrats

Hazards: Though minimal on the beginner loop, watch for exposed tree roots, rocks, and logs. There are many potential hazards (challenges) on the expert loop. Watch for poison ivy, prickly ash (sharp thorns), and wild parsnip (a tall weed that will inflict ebola-like wounds upon exposed skin).

Other considerations: Trail will close if conditions pose harm to riders. Keep the soft tread in top shape by postponing your ride after rains or spring snow.

Maps: *DeLorme: Minnesota Atlas & Gazetteer* map 76; Three River Parks map: www .threeriversparks.org/activities/mountain-biking.aspx

Getting there: From I-35 W in Burnsville, follow CR 42 west 2 miles to W. Burnsville Parkway. Turn south past Cam Ram Park to Hanrehan Lake Boulevard and continue to Murphy Lake Road, a left turn onto gravel. The trailhead is at the top of the hill. GPS: N44° 43.456' / W93° 20.927'

The Ride

One of the first metro area parks to ordain mountain bike–specific trails, Murphy-Hanrehan's early paths were created prior to the sensible trend of sustainable trail building. Often rutted or eroding, the trails charged up and down hills and shot through the woods with little regard to fall lines or harmonious relations with the natural terrain. While still a fun and challenging ride, clearer heads prevailed and relocated the entire mountain bike trail system to the park's southern meadows and oak forest. Murphy's 2,800 acres are generally split into steep, wooded hills and scattered wetlands in the northern section, and the

Riding in NICK PETTIS

aforementioned oak stands and prairie restoration in the southern sections. All that adds up to a remote wilderness vibe and close-in escape from surrounding frenetic life.

From the trailhead, the path cuts between two signs loaded with great park and riding info, and heads into open prairie to start the beginner loop (intermediate and expert loops are only accessed via the easy loop, so more accomplished riders can use this as a warm-up). This entry loop has been redesigned to accommodate adaptive mountain bikes and hand cycles. Keep your eyes peeled for soaring raptors like red-shouldered and Cooper's hawks scanning for a meal. Roll across the prairie and drop into the oak-laden woods on the intermediate loop, starting out over some rocks between the trees and a log crossing,

The Billy Goat Bridge, an old wooden railroad bridge in the area of Judicial Road and Burnsville Parkway, was a main conduit for the comings and goings of residents in the townships south of Minneapolis, carrying horse-drawn sleighs and Model Ts to the post office, school, and church. The name was inspired by a group of billy goats from a neighboring farm that had a merry old time running back and forth across the bridge.

FOR THE BIRDS

The diverse habitats at Murphy-Hanrehan are home to over one hundred breeding bird species, and the National Audubon Society has listed the park as an Important Bird Area, which provides essential habitat for nesting birds. Murphy is the only known nesting location in Minnesota for hooded warblers. Other uncommon species found in this pocket wilderness are American redstarts, ovenbirds, wood thrushes, and scarlet tanagers. This is also a critical migratory stopover for forest songbirds, with regular species counts of twenty-five warblers per day.

then into some tight singletrack. The path follows a hairpin west, with an easy climb and a tour along the contours of the glacial ridge. Two more tight hairpin turns lead southeast to the junction with the expert loop. Ride across the boardwalk to the edge of the wetland, take in sweet views of the beauteous landscape, and follow the rolling path along the wetland back to the easy loop junction and final stretch to the trailhead.

Minnesota meadow NICK PETTIS

Sunbeam turn on sweet singletrack NICK PETTIS

The expert loop boasts some of the sweetest singletrack around on a 7-mile carnival ride with high and narrow bridges, skinnier tread on steep sideslopes, bigger climbs and faster descents, and cool obstacles like the 45-foot-long ladder bridge and log ride. There are six total bridges and a few boardwalks peppered along the loop, making for great fun all the way through, and a few sections of open prairie, typically with wildlife all over the place, like deer, rabbits, fox, woodchucks, and raptors. Even just one lap provides a worthy challenge, but can you really resist doing another one?

Miles and Directions

0.0   Setting out from the trailhead, start the beginner loop to the left. The path meanders through the meadow on a back-and-forth route that generally forms a loop.

0.9   Junction with the intermediate loop. Follow the path toward the left, directly into the woods on the skinnier trail with more steep sections and technical trail.

Murphy–Hanrehan Park Reserve

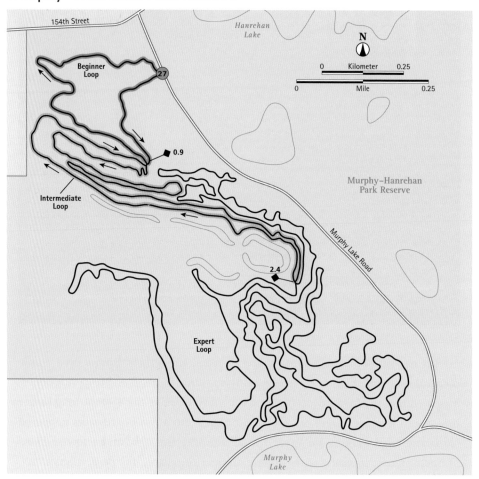

2.4 Junction with the expert loop. To complete the featured route, ride across the
    boardwalk and roll back through the woods, north then westerly, hit the easy loop
    again, and head back to the trailhead. (*Option:* At the junction with the expert loop,
    keep heading south for the really good stuff.)

3.5 Arrive back at the trailhead.

Ride Information

Restaurants: All manner of food stops are available just a few miles away on the Burnsville Center strip of CR 42, including the obligatory Starbucks and Caribou coffee shops, a plethora of fast-food joints, and plenty of "sit down" restaurants.

Local Events and Attractions: Freewheel Bike hosts a three-day mountain bike camp at Murphy in August. Their fat tire team imparts sage wisdom of the basics of singletrack riding, safety, position, and more. Check threeriversparks.org for registration info.

Get to Murphy for the racing in August and September. Cosponsored by Three Rivers Parks and REI, the 10K race is always a blast, and there are prizes! See threeriversparks .org for information.

—Steve Johnson

28 Lebanon Hills

MORC's flagship trail and one of Minnesota's very best, Lebanon Hills is 100 percent singletrack bliss. The superbly designed trail system treats riders to 10 (and count-ing) miles of sinuous turns, rock gardens, log piles, bridges, open meadow, and dense woods. Anyone from beginner to expert can sample the wares on four connected loops, nested in a pattern of steadily increasing difficulty. The racing action here is always a blast, even deep into the winter.

Start: Trailhead on Johnny Cake Ridge Road

Distance: 5 miles

Riding time: Plan on around 1 hour, but stay for more

Terrain and surface type: Rolling, with short, punchy climbs and one long grind, all on hardpacked singletrack

Highlights: All of the above if you so desire, sublime singletrack throughout, excel-lent variety of trails, great scenery

Hazards: Stacked inventory of rock gardens, log crossings, jumps, narrow bridges, and other optional challenges

Other considerations: Trail gets crowded, especially on weekends

Maps: *DeLorme: Minnesota Atlas & Gazetteer* map 71; excellent map resources at morcmtb.org

Getting there: From I-35, exit at Cliff Road, head east 0.7 mile to Johnny Cake Ridge Road, and turn south. Parking and trailhead 0.5 mile in on west side of road. GPS: N44° 46.974' / W93° 11.283'

The Ride

This is where it all started. Minnesota's rise to a top mountain-biking destination in the country first percolated in this little pocket of woods in a county park. Eroding trails, off-camber turns, and unstable tread were transformed, with an arsenal of earth-sculpting tools wielded by scores of dedicated volunteers, into a trail system so masterfully designed that it is now a showcase after which many other trails are modeled. Sustainably built trails weave seamlessly into the natu-ral contours of the woods, flowing up and around hills and ponds and over strate-gically placed obstacles. The trails are flowing and fast, and arranged in a way that allows both newer riders to hone their skills and advanced riders to challenge themselves on the more difficult inner courses. Many years in the making, the

A challenging trail obstacle in the Lebanon Hills STEVE JOHNSON

hard work put into these trails really shines. *Red alert:* By the time you read this, a new trailhead "complex" will have opened to accommodate Leb's overwhelming popularity, with ample parking, restrooms, changing rooms, picnic shelter, and posted trail maps. Adjacent to the trailhead is a new skills park.

The beginner loop, and ultimately all loops, starts from the northwest corner of the parking lot with a gentle climb through a small stand of pines. There are a few bypass sections where you can try your bike-handling skills, or play it safe and stick to the main trail. A fast-paced downhill leads to an optional log jump, and a quick pass over the cross-country ski trail blends into open, flowy single-track with enough tight turns to keep it lively.

Start the intermediate and expert (or X) loops from the same spot, but ride west on Dream II, up through the pines on one of the longest climbs in the park (about 0.25 mile) and in some of the most handsome scenery. The trail moves along to some tricky rock gardens, a double jump, and then a fun descent to the Joey Trail. This is my personal favorite stretch of the loop, with a fast and winding path over just enough rocks and roots to elicit a few hoots and hollers. The path squiggles south, then turns east to the Stooges Run, a collection of tightly packed turns with a log pile and switchbacks leading to the Bypass climb, another

ONION KING

Did you know that Eagan was once the Onion Capital of the United States? Around the time of Eagan Township's establishment in 1860, farmland dominated the sprawling landscape, and most residents were, naturally, farmers tending to various crops. The late 1800s must have sparked an interest in onions, when the bulbous plant was grown in earnest and shipped all over the country. Poor harvest years and stiff competition from southern states ended Eagan's onion reign around 1930.

long grind to some nice views on the Upper Bypass trail, looping around the top of the hill and through some tricky rock gardens to a descent to the big, spoked trail junction. The intermediate path continues east on more excellent single-track, some manageable rock gardens, and even a cool rock jump as it winds back and forth in a bunch of finger loops to a pond, and the last section blasts around banked turns, more fast descents, and a challenging, three-tiered climb to the final descent. One of the newer sections is like a BMX track with rolling jumps and other technical features. It's super fun to ride on a mountain bike, and it seems to bring others, like freestyle riders, out to give it a try and nail some airborne tricks.

The X and XX Loops are just that—for experts and even better experts. The X includes tons of log piles to shimmy over and a handful of fun rock sections, with some that serve up a healthy technical challenge, like the bermed turn of Tedman's Curve. Some S turns lead up to a high point in the park, followed by a killer descent with a couple of log jumps to a bypass trail reconnection to the intermediate loop. Or hang a left and test your mettle on the XX Loop, featuring some of the most rugged terrain in the area, like rock-strewn hill climbs, narrow wooden bridges, a camelback feature, log stair-step climbs, and screaming descents with bermed corners. And don't miss the log ladder leading to a fun rock obstacle. The XX is a tough trail, but a genuine blast to ride.

Martin Diffley started a roadside vegetable stand in Eagan in 1973, ushering in a passionate commitment to organic farming on the family's farmland. The Diffley family continues to cultivate sustainable farming and growing practices through workshops, consulting, and public events. organicfarmingworks.com

Miles and Directions

0.0 Start at the trailhead, heading west.

0.9 Follow the Dream II trail until you merge onto the Joey Trail.

1.5 Hit the twists and turns of Stooges Run.

2.0 Climb up Bypass, and curve around Upper Bypass.

2.5 Junction with expert (X and XX) loops. Hang a right to continue Intermediate loop.

5.0 Arrive back at the trailhead.

Lebanon Hills

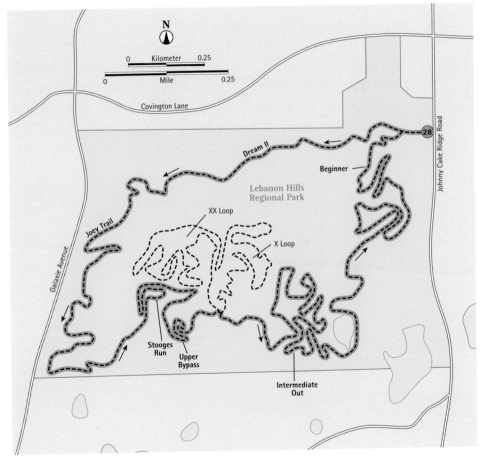

Ride Information

Restaurants: How does a big ol' malt sound after a hot summer trail ride? Dairy Queen is only about a mile away. 4630 Rahncliff Road, Eagan; (651) 688-2725; dairyqueen.com

> Pizza and brew are a tasty conclusion to your ride. Grab a table at Green Mill, 1940 Rahncliff Ct., Eagan; (651) 686-7166; greenmill.com

Local Events and Attractions: Lebanon Hills Regional Park is packed with opportunities to get outside, like the parent-child kayak days, and the Lost in the Woods wilderness camps; 860 Cliff Road, Eagan; co.dakota.mn.us

—Steve Johnson

29 Elm Creek Fat Tire Trails

Three Rivers Park District and MORC boast 13 miles of sublime singletrack at Elm Creek Park Reserve, twisting around the northeast corner of the park through dense hardwood forest and open prairie, with a perfectly blended mix of beginner to expert terrain on a fast-flowing path with only rare unintended obstacles. Decadent paved trails through the rest of the wildlife-packed park add bonus points.

Start: At parking area across from dog park on Goose Lake Road

Distance: 7.5 miles

Riding time: 1 to 1.5 hours

Terrain and surface type: Flat to gently rolling on hardpacked singletrack

Highlights: Impeccable trail conditions, fast and flowing, gorgeous scenery, relatively crowd-free

Hazards: Hardly an exposed root or stray branch to be seen; very worry-free trail

Maps: *DeLorme: Minnesota Atlas & Gazetteer* map 70; Three Rivers Parks map www .threeriversparks.org/parks/elm-creek-park/elm-creek-singletrack-trail.aspx

Getting there: From I-94, take exit 213 for Maple Grove Parkway toward CR 30. Turn right onto Maple Grove Parkway and head northeast for 1.3 miles. Turn right onto CR 81, heading southeast. Take the very next left to turn north onto Fernbrook Lane. After 1.1 miles turn right onto Elm Creek Road. In about 3.0 miles reach the Dog Park trailhead parking area at Goose Lake Road. GPS: N45° 10.113' / W93° 25.324'

The Ride

I double-dipped on my Elm Creek day and rode both the paved and dirt trails, so this route starts from the dog park trailhead. Follow the road north to the junction with the paved trail and hop on the singletrack, cruising through an open, meadowy landscape to a short climb through a chunk of woods, then squiggle around through the open again to meet the access to Grizzland, the expert section dotted with technical features like log piles and rock gardens, and boasting the most elevation gain on the trail. It's a blast in there, but for now we'll focus on a broader, intermediate skill level (like mine) and ride to the east on the mid-level trail, curving through a splintered copse of trees, into the open again, and back into a large tract of woods near Lemans Lake. The path continues this trees-to-clearing-to-trees pattern northbound along a small rise, then drops gradually

Riding the stump bridge NICK PETTIS

down to the northern trailhead. Curve around to the south and roll up and down through beautiful oak-maple-basswood forest on a fast and flowing stretch past a small pond and meadow. A "big" climb of about 70 feet takes you through more forest and around a huge meadow area to the final roller-coaster but straight finish.

If you'd like to ride longer, the park has 6.5 more miles of trail. The two easier loops at Elm Creek, totaling a little over 2 miles, offer something you don't see every day on a mountain-bike trail. The trails were designed to accommodate the wide wheelbase of three- and four-wheeled adaptive mountain bikes and hand cycles. Grades are not typically more than 5 percent, although a 900-foot-long ascent will challenge riders on the western loop. The park and MORC volunteers have done a fantastic job of constructing this trail and providing access for yet another active group of cyclists. This trail and one at Murphy-Hanrehan in Savage are two of the very few hand-cycle trails in the country, and Dan Fjell, outdoor

Elm Creek Fat Tire Trails

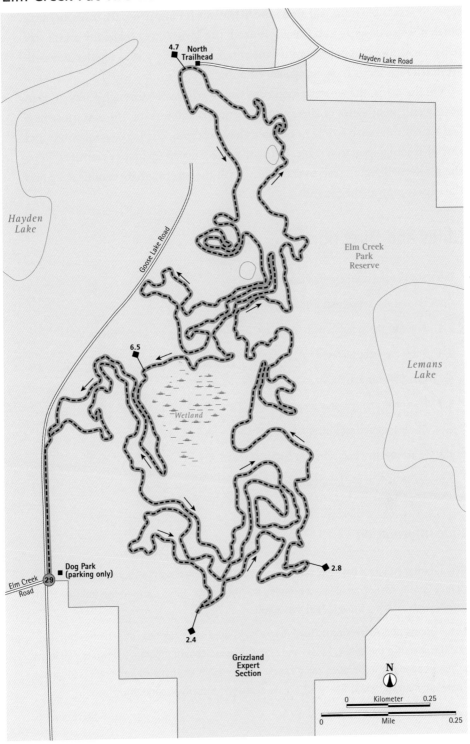

recreation specialist at Three Rivers Parks, is enthusiastic for future plans: "These types of accessible trails will always be in the mix for any new park trails, because of what we've done at Elm Creek." Indeed, the Twin Cities is already on its way to be the Midwest hub for adaptive mountain-bike trails, with a regular and well-attended race series happening every summer.

On the trails, the western loop runs counterclockwise through a mix of open prairie and great views of surrounding wetlands and forests. The eastern loop is less than 1 mile with barely noticeable elevation gain, circling several ponds and tracing a squiggly, glacial ridge. Both are perfect warm-up loops prior to tackling the more challenging trail to the south, with the intermediate trail next up and the expert loop at the far end.

Miles and Directions

0.0 Start at the southern trailhead.

0.2 Hop on the singletrack leading north from the bike path.

2.4 Arrive at the junction with Grizzland. Turn left to follow the intermediate trail.

2.8 Enter the woods on east side of park.

4.7 Pass the northern trailhead.

5.4 Pass pond and meadow area.

6.5 Circle around west side of a huge, Wisconsin-shaped wetland.

7.3 Reach the junction with bike path and road.

7.5 Arrive back at the trailhead.

Ride Information

Restaurants: Pull up a bar stool and devour a plate of french toast or burgers and fries at Dehn's County Manor, an all-in-the-family tradition since 1958. Close to the trails at 11281 Fernbrook Ln., Maple Grove; (763) 420-6460.

Local Events and Attractions: Three Rivers Parks host a full calendar of activities throughout the year, like the canoe, kayak, and stand-up paddleboard programs. Newbies can learn different paddling techniques, roll a kayak, and see what the paddleboard craze is all about. There are many different flavors of events available; threeriversparks.org.

—Steve Johnson

30 Salem Hills Trails

This 4.5-mile linear trail at Harmon Park cruises a mellow course through wildflower-packed meadows and pine-hardwood forest on smooth, flowing, and gently rolling singletrack. It's the perfect place for new riders to get comfortable and gain confidence, and advanced riders can appreciate an easy trail day or speed workout.

Start: Trailhead at end of Asher Avenue

Distance: 4.5 miles for three linked loops

Riding time: About 30 minutes

Terrain and surface type: Gently rolling on smooth, hardpacked singletrack

Highlights: Gorgeous scenery, low to moderate technical level and just-right distance for new riders, all on a stacked loop system, great ski trails in winter

Hazards: None

Maps: *DeLorme: Minnesota Atlas & Gazetteer* map 71; MORC maps at morcmtb.org

Getting there: From I-494, exit MN 3 (S. Robert Trail) and head south 0.2 mile to Upper 55th Street. Turn left after 0.5 mile onto Asher Avenue and head south to the trailhead. GPS: N°44 51.925' / W93° 04.403'

The Ride

Don't let the short mileage at Salem Hills fool you. Every inch of the park's 4.5 miles is on sublime singletrack and is so addicting, plan on extra time to get your multiple lap fix. Salem's three linked loops offer a nice mix of scenery, with a woodsy start giving way to open prairie, a small pond, and a handful of bridge crossings. This is also a regular locale for the launch of the Minnesota Mountain Bike Series, and despite the absence of a lung-busting climb or white-knuckle downhill, many racers say it's their favorite event of the year.

Start the ride heading north into the woods on the Singletrack Sawmill, other aliases being the North Loop or North Forks Trail, with just under a mile of snaky singletrack as fine as any you'll find in the metro area. Loop around and back to the south, rolling through prairie grasses and wildflowers (don't miss the in-season blackberries), past the entrance trail, to the Pond Loop, introduced by a high-speed banked corner that ejects you into rolling pine forest mixed with prairie grass. If rain has fallen within the past few days, this would be the most likely spot to encounter a puddle or two, as it is a sometimes soggy section. A short bridge crossing past the pond leads up a little hill to the junction with the

Singletrack snaking through the meadows STEVE JOHNSON

South (Prairie Fire) Loop. Sweep across gorgeous Minnesota prairie planted with native grasses and wildflowers, and be on the lookout for bluebirds frolicking about. The trail leaves the prairie and moves into a hammerhead section in the woods, then a few more prairie-to-woods-to-prairie transitions leading to the far southern part of the park. Loop back north along the fringe of the woods and back into another fun stretch of meadow to the top of the loop, and turn left into the woods for the west side of the Pond Loop, a flat cruise to one more bridge and more open country riding. Salem's one obstacle, a big ol' boulder wedged in the path, appears near the top of the loop. Conquer the rock and ride around to the final turn back to the trailhead.

INVER GROVE'S ROOTS

German and Irish settlers filtered into the rolling hills and verdant country-side of present-day Inver Grove Heights around 1852, incorporating into a township six years later. Their young village was named after "Inver," an Irish fishing village, and "Grove," the German settlers' homeland.

Salem Hills Trails

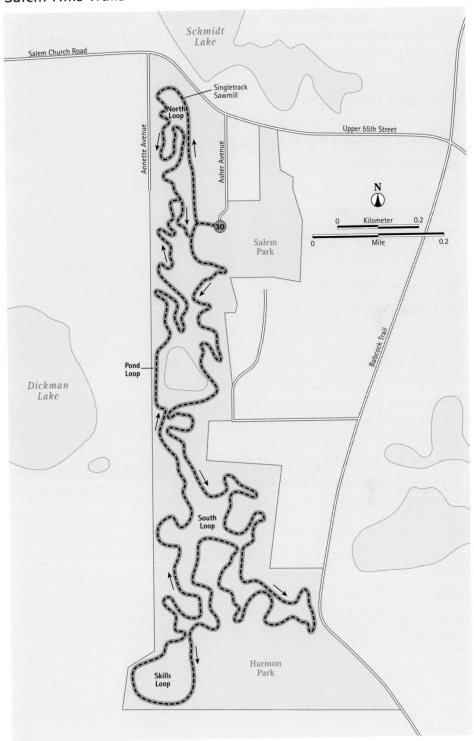

Groovy trail rep: Salem Hills exists thanks to a team effort between MORC and the city of Inver Grove Heights, when the park won a place on the International Mountain Biking Association's (IMBA) 2003 Hot Spots program, a nationwide effort focusing on building singletrack in urban areas across the country.

Miles and Directions

0.0   Start at the trailhead. Ride north on a counterclockwise loop.

0.7   Reach the junction with the top end of the Pond Loop. Stay left, then right to start the loop.

1.0   Ride past the pond and over a bridge.

1.2   Turn right to start the South Loop.

3.4   Arrive back at the top of South Loop and continue on the west side of Pond Loop.

3.9   Reach the junction with North Loop. Go right to finish the lap.

4.5   Return back to the trailhead.

Ride Information

Restaurants: You can't beat a giant burrito and frosty beverage after a great trail day. Fill up at Chipotle, just up the road at 1857 S. Ritobert St., West Saint Paul; (651) 552-2110; chipotle.com.

Local Events and Attractions: Trade your bike for running shoes and see Salem's trails at a slower pace at the Harmon Farms Trail Runs, mid-September at Harmon Park (aka Salem Hills); invergroveheights.org.

—Steve Johnson

31 Battle Creek Regional Park

Battle Creek Regional Park is often included in lists detailing the best trails to ride in the state of Minnesota—not just in the Twin Cities. That's probably because there's a beautiful mixture of dense oak forest and open meadows with substantial flora and fauna that you'd never expect to find so close to urbanity. Here we take you through 4 of the 10 total trail miles available, dancing amidst the 750 acres that make up this park.

Start: On the singletrack directly south of Battle Creek Community Center, 75 S. Winthrop St.

Distance: 4.2-mile loop

Riding time: 45 to 60 minutes

Terrain and surface type: Hilly with a mixture of climbs and steep descents over packed singletrack

Highlights: A very twisty trail with a healthy blend of rolling meadows and climbs in dense woods throughout this challenging ride

Hazards: Sandy portions, exposed roots and logs

Map: *DeLorme: Minnesota Atlas & Gazetteer* map 71

Getting there: From downtown Saint Paul, drive east on I-94 about 5 miles to McKnight Road. Go right (south) to Upper Afton Road and turn right again onto Winthrop Street. Go left; just 1 block, turn right into the Battle Creek Community Center. The trailhead is at the southwest end of the lot. GPS: N44° 56.315' / W93° 00.766'

The Ride

Here's the deal, folks. If you don't think you should be riding on the mountain-biking equivalent of a black diamond—take extreme caution on this trail. The arteries in my left leg wish I had.

If you do any reading about riding in Battle Creek Regional Park, you'll likely find a couple of things. First, trail review website singletracks.com gives this ride an "advanced" rating with a little black diamond over it. User reviews largely concur.

But also signage is—at least up to the time of riding for this book—notoriously lacking. Almost anyone who has taken his or her bike out to Battle Creek recommends only doing it with someone who knows where he or she is going.

Top side turn with Mississippi River in background STEVE JOHNSON

Luckily I was once again with Porter. But unfortunately, I was with Porter.

Of all the disciplines covered in this book, mountain biking is admittedly my weakest. So I should have known better before going as hard as I did at Battle Creek. I thought I was taking it easy, opting to walk certain, rockier sections that I presumed to be above my skill level.

Porter, meanwhile, was a kid on the playground.

Then, following a steep descent that I took slowly, I allowed myself to gain a little speed. I could see the wooden bridge approaching.

Well, I smacked my left handlebar into a small tree as I whizzed by. This sent me flying out of the saddle—a common enough maneuver among the mountain-biking community. Unfortunately, that left handlebar turned sharply and hit me right in the groin. (Not *that* part of the groin. The world can still be blessed with future copies of myself, if my wife and I are ever so inclined.)

My left side immediately went numb as I grunted through the worst pain of my life. Porter turned back and did the best he could to assist me. We waited for some time, but it seemed best to call it a day.

I spent the rest of the day and night icing. It looked like a normal bruise, after all. Yet when I tried to go for a simple walk around the block, my left leg became useless, as if I just had done 1,000 squats. A couple days later, I finally made a doctor's appointment. Upon noticing that my left foot was especially white, even for my computer-paper skin tone, I was hastily sent off to the emergency room where I would receive arterial surgery the next day. Turned out I had punctured a small hole in one of my arteries, and blood simply wasn't getting where it needed to go.

To summarize, I rode a course beyond my skill level, and now I have pieces of cow heart in one of my arteries.

For those who can tackle a difficult course without puncturing an artery (or even those who have a better sense of when to slow down), Battle Creek is a lovely mixture of rolling singletrack with a number of loops that work their way through dense woodland. Of course you get those steep climbs and descents, considering this used to be a downhill ski joint.

From the trailhead, follow the singletrack to the southwest on a sinuous roll-out along the cross-country ski trail's lighted section of paths. At the far end of the ski trails, the singletrack enters a stand of tall pines and then the thicker woods of the park at the first junction. Do a little zig and climb the access "road" (ski path) up to the top of the hill. Follow the ski sign to the left, rolling through gorgeous oak forest with good views of the Mississippi River here and there through the trees. Pass a small meadow frequented by white-tailed deer, and at the meadow's far edge, shoot left on the partially hidden singletrack into the

SKI JUMPING ANYONE?

Once upon a time, the 60-meter ski jump at Battle Creek Park was one of the largest in the world as jumpers first started hitting the slopes in the late 1930s. Nearby Mounds Park boasted Saint Paul's first jumping hill, but it was destroyed when a wind storm collapsed the structure in 1939, leading to a replacement at Battle Creek. The jump was completed in time for that year's Saint Paul Winter Carnival and national ski-jumping championships. This Battle Creek jump survived into the 1970s when a new 40-meter hill was established at the southern edge of Maplewood. The Saint Paul Ski Club uses it to this day.

A jumping program is available, catering to beginners and experts. Once the warm weather returns, the Saint Paul Ski Club reverts to summer jumping on synthetic-surfaced hills. Visit stpaulskiclub.com for more info.

woods. This is a blast of a downhill with mini jumps and berms and rocks. Keep your head up and watch your speed as you near the bottom; the steep drop is prime turf to go over the bars.

At the bottom, fork left over a short, steep hump and loop back east along Lower Afton Road. The trail climbs along the contour line through a mini pine and aspen forest, then back into the deeper woods. Follow the singletrack sign into a deep bowl carpeted with emerald green ferns and purple flower accents in spring. Here the trail loops around the bowl, up and down bumps with dense foliage all around. At the next junction, go straight up the hill and back to the original intersection near the ski trails. Go straight on, up to the ridge above the community center and descend the other side to a left turn into the woods again. Take that immediate right and descend gradually to a T junction. A right turn here heads along a fun, twisty course through sprig aspen and oak, eventually descending to another T at Battle Creek Road. Take a short jog right and back onto the dirt singletrack leading into the park's western section.

Pass several junctions from the right dropping down to Battle Creek, and to the left is a bowl of a former pond. Continue counterclockwise, listening for the train whistles from the Canadian Pacific yard at the river below. Check out the

Resident wildlife STEVE JOHNSON

Battle Creek Regional Park

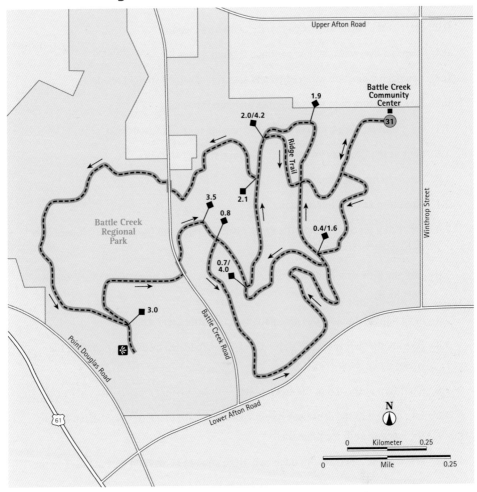

Upper Afton Road

Battle Creek Community Center

1.9

2.0/4.2

Ridge Trail

3.5   2.1

0.8

0.4/1.6

Battle Creek Regional Park

0.7/ 4.0

3.0

Point Douglas Road

Battle Creek Road

Winthrop Street

Lower Afton Road

61

N

| 0 | Kilometer | 0.25 |
| 0 | Mile | 0.25 |

spur path leading to the crest of the hill for sweet views of the river valley. Head back toward the "lake" and take a right turn along a straight, old roadbed to Battle Creek Road, jog left, and ride back into the woods. An immediate right turn heads up a short but ste-e-e-e-ep climb to a T junction, and more climbing to the right back up past the meadow. This time take a left into the oaks on smooth singletrack. Keep taking right turns and you climb steadily to the top of the hill and the exit back to the parking area.

Miles and Directions

0.0 Start at the Battle Creek Community Center trailhead.

0.4 There's a five-way junction; continue straight across.

0.7 Approach a junction with right-hand spur trail. Keep on straight ahead.

0.8 Take a left turn onto the singletrack and into the woods.

1.1 Hit a turn heading back northeast and parallel to Lower Afton Road.

1.6 Back at the five-way intersection, continue straight through.

1.9 Turn left into the woods.

2.1 Right turn at the T intersection.

2.4 Arrive at a junction with Battle Creek Road. Go right and take a quick left back into the woods.

3.0 Take the little spur trail to the edge of the bluff to enjoy great views of the Mississippi River.

3.3 Bend right and follow the wide path back to Battle Creek Road.

3.4 Take another left turn onto Battle Creek Road, followed by a quick right into the woods again.

3.5 Right turn at the top of the steep climb.

4.0 Take a left into the dense oak forest. Follow the path uphill to a right-hand fork to the junction with the ridge trail.

4.2 Arrive at the junction with ridge trail. Head straight across and descend back to the trailhead.

32 Mendota Trail—Eagan

The pan-flat companion to Elm Creek Fat Tire Trails' up-and-down affair, this 12-mile out-and-back follows the Minnesota River's southern banks on a mix of single- and doubletrack on a mostly wooded trail heading through Fort Snelling State Park's wildlife-rich river flats.

> Start: Trailhead parking area on MN 13 in Mendota, just east of Saint Peter's Church
>
> Distance: 12-mile out and back
>
> Riding time: About 1.5 hours
>
> Terrain and surface type: Flat singletrack and doubletrack on hardpacked and sandy trail
>
> Highlights: Close-up river views; herons, ducks, deer, raptors; Henry Sibley House
>
> Hazards: Occasional downed tree limbs, sections of deep sand and waterlogged trail, watch for hikers
>
> Other considerations: Steer clear of the trail when wet to avoid damage to the route.
>
> Map: *DeLorme: Minnesota Atlas & Gazetteer* map 70
>
> Getting there: From MN 55 at the Mendota Bridge, follow MN 110 on the south side of the river westward to the stoplight at MN 13. Go left (north) and follow the curves past Saint Peter's Church to the parking lot on the left side of the road, on the hill above downtown Mendota. GPS: N44° 53.241' / W93° 09.907'

The Ride

This ride starts in the shadow of Minnesota's oldest church, in one of the state's oldest towns, overlooking homesites of two of the most influential people in Minnesota's history: Henry Sibley and Jean Baptiste Faribault. Longtime home of the Dakota Indians, the Mendota area also attracted the first white settlers to the young Minnesota Territory, jump-started by a bustling fur trade headquartered in this very spot. Roll through this time warp with a warm-up spin through Mendota's 2-block main street (MN 13) and drop down the hill on D Street past the historic Sibley house (see sidebar). The stone arch tunnel beneath the Canadian Pacific railroad line leads to Fort Snelling State Park land and the Mendota Trail. The Mississippi River is dead ahead, taking in water from the Minnesota River only a few hundred yards upstream. Ride west on wide hardpack, crossing

Trailside maintenance by resident beavers STEVE JOHNSON

a few intermittent mini streams born of runoff from snow or rain, below the cement rainbow arches of the Mendota Bridge. Now paralleling the Minnesota River, a brief section of open grassland gives way to thick woods of elm, maple, and cottonwood, their dense canopy shading an impenetrable green flood of assorted shrubbery and ground-level foliage in summer. Heed not the call of nature in this section, lest the plethora of stinging nettles and poison ivy leave their mark on your . . . ride. And speaking of floods, this long ribbon of the river valley has been submerged many a wet spring, leaving dead fish hanging from tree branches and deep dunes of murky river sediment. The rising river will, of course, change the complexion of the trail, so plan accordingly and ride somewhere else when wet to keep trail damage at bay.

The Dakota named the joining of the Minnesota and Mississippi Rivers *mdo-te*, or "meeting of the waters." It was a place of great spiritual and cultural significance for the Dakota and Ojibwa people for hundreds of years. Hike here on the Pike Island trail from the Fort Snelling State Park Visitor Center.

Riding along the riverbank, nearly at water level, the trail passes beneath the flight path for Minneapolis–Saint Paul International Airport, and you have a good vantage for examining the underbellies of jets roaring over your head. At around the 3-mile mark, the path

S-curves under the dual span of I-494 and darts arrow-straight on a boulevard-like path shadowed by an awning of giant trees. At the end of the tree tunnel, the trail morphs into singletrack and shimmies between conveniently spaced riverbank trees, with a huge expanse of wetland meadow to the south. The natural environment and wildlife habitat here share that of the Minnesota Valley National Wildlife Refuge land directly across the river. With one of only four urban wildlife refuges in the country, we are fortunate to have this gem so close to home. Stretching along 99 miles of the Minnesota River in 14 linear units, the refuge provides critical habitat to over 200 bird species and other critters like white-tailed deer, red fox, and snapping turtles, thriving in marshland, lakes, remnant oak savanna, and floodplain forest.

Five bridge crossings provide safe passage over river tributaries and other soggy sections, and at times the trail is simply whatever path best travels among the changing tide of sand and river debris. Don't be surprised if you're blocked altogether by high water at a few points along this stretch, but during summer and fall, it's mostly smooth sailing. The trees abruptly give way to tall shrubs,

HENRY SIBLEY

In the still-wild northern frontier of a young country, the American Fur Company established a trading post near Fort Snelling, across the confluence of the Minnesota and Mississippi Rivers. Known as the "Sioux Outfit," the post provided the impetus for the settlement and founding of Mendota, one of Minnesota's first towns. At the helm of the trading center was Henry Sibley, an ambitious young man pivotal in the fur company's success and in maintaining robust relations with the Dakota Indians. Named "Walker in the Pines" by the Dakota, Sibley lived on-site while pursuing political aspirations, thrice serving as congressional delegate and affording key input in drafting Minnesota's constitution. He was a military commander during the Dakota War, accomplished businessman, and president of both the Minnesota Historical Society and University of Minnesota Board of Regents, and he published volumes of work on the state's history. During his tenure as Minnesota's first governor, Sibley kept an office in the 1835 stone house in Mendota, where he lived until 1862, when he moved with his family to Saint Paul. Tour the house on weekends from late May to early Sept. Admission fee for adults. 1357 Sibley Memorial Hwy., Mendota 55120; (651) 452-1596; mnhs.org

then just tall grasses on the last section of wide, fast trail to the Cedar Avenue bridge. ***Notes from here:*** The bike/ped bridge ramps up and parallels the buzz of the highway to the north side of the river. In the old days, you could cruise along Old Cedar Avenue and cross the equally old, wood-planked bridge into Bloomington. Deemed unsafe and closed in 2002, the span was closed and the planks removed, demolition imminent. However, progress is (sort of) being made between the multiple agencies involved to either renovate the existing 1920s bridge, build a new one, or come up with some other way to get across Long Meadow Lake. Meantime, if you are aboard a mountain bike, eyeball the skinny singletrack right on the riverbank, adjacent to the bike ramp. This little number

Mendota Trail–Eagan

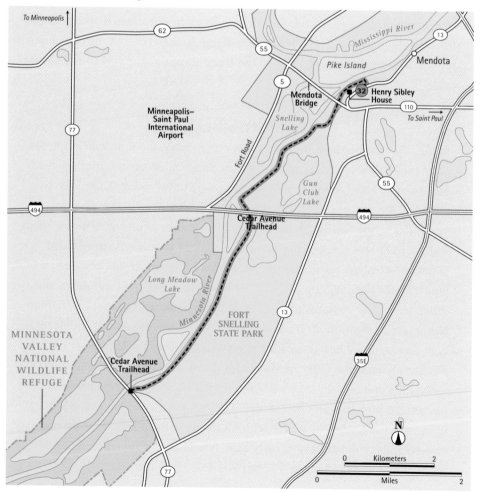

snakes through 8-foot-tall grass and all manner of encroaching foliage to eventually join the start of the Bloomington side of the river trails. A pretty cool, Huck-Finn-on-a-bike kind of adventure.

Miles and Directions

0.0 Start at Mendota trailhead on MN 13.

0.3 Head under the railroad tunnel into Fort Snelling State Park.

0.7 Pass under MN 55.

1.2 Trail meets and parallels the Minnesota River.

3.0 Pass under I-494.

6.0 Arrive at junction with Cedar Avenue trailhead. Turn around to retrace the route.

12.0 Arrive back at the trailhead.

Option: To make this a 6-mile one-way ride, arrange for someone to pick you up at the Cedar Avenue trailhead or leave a car there. From MN 77 (Cedar Avenue), exit MN 13 northbound. In 0.25 mile, turn left at Silver Bell Road. Follow Silver Bell Road down to the Minnesota River. The parking area is on your right, directly beneath the Cedar Avenue bridge. The trail is at the east end of the parking area.

Ride Information

Restaurants: Lucky's 13 Pub serves up good times and great food, with the Big Rivers Regional Trail right out the back door. 1352 Sibley Memorial Hwy., Mendota; (651) 452-0161; luckys13pub.com

Local Events and Attractions: One of Minnesota's oldest cities gets its groove on in early July at Mendota Days with a parade, live music, and special attractions like the rolling heroics of the Twin Cities Unicycle Club. The action happens on Sibley Memorial Highway (MN 13) in Mendota. mendotaheights.patch.com

—Steve Johnson

PADDLING

The Twin Cities might not be the first region you think of when it comes to paddling. Then you realize Minnesota *is* the "Land of 10,000 Lakes." Of course there's great paddling to be had here!

Here we have five lake paddles within and around the Twin Cities plus three river paddles, only one of which requires a significant car ride. Sara Woodruff of Silver Creek Paddle joined me for a number of the paddles and loaned some of her expertise on what to include and leave out.

Grab a board and get in the water. You'll be glad that you did.

As we drift toward Psycho Suzi's along the Mississippi River, the Minneapolis skyline starts to twinkle in the early summer evening. JOE BAUR

33 Mississippi River

A paddle on the Mississippi River is essential for any local or visiting paddler. Best of all, it's far more welcoming than many might believe, especially considering the crashing falls one sees from Stone Arch Bridge. In reality, this section of the Mississippi River can be as surprisingly pristine and manageable as any other paddle in the book. We work our way south from Coon Rapids Dam Regional Park in the suburb of the same name down to the dock at Psycho Suzi's Motor Lounge (a tiki-themed restaurant) in Minneapolis's Nordeast neighborhood.

Start: Coon Rapids Dam Regional Park

End: Psycho Suzi's Motor Lounge

Distance: 10 miles

Float time: 2 hours

Difficulty rating: Moderate due to distance

Current: Slow to moderate

Nearest city/town: Coon Rapids, Minneapolis

Boats used: Canoe, kayak, johnboat, small motorized craft, stand-up paddleboard

Getting there: To takeout: From Minneapolis, cross the Mississippi River to get to University Avenue SE. Take University Avenue SE to Broadway Street NE and turn left. In 0.3 mile, turn right onto Marshall Street NE for 0.6 mile. Psycho Suzi's Motor Lounge will be on the left. 1900 Marshall St NE, Minneapolis, MN 55418

From Saint Paul, drive west on I-94 toward Minneapolis. Take exit 235B for Huron Boulevard. In 0.1 mile, turn left onto University Avenue SE. Turn left onto Broadway Street NE and follow for 0.3 mile; turn right onto Marshall Street NE for 0.6 mile. Psycho Suzi's Motor Lounge will be on the left.

To put-in from takeout: From Psycho Suzi's Motor Lounge, get back on Marshall St NE, turning left to head north. Turn left in 0.4 mile onto the Lowry Bridge and take the first right onto N. 2nd Street after crossing the Mississippi River. Continue north as N. 2nd Street turns into N. Washington Avenue and follow signs for I-94 W. Take I-94 W north for 2.9 miles to MN 252 N and continue on MN 252 driving north for 2 miles. Turn off to the right at 77th Avenue N/Brookdale Drive and take a quick left onto W. River Road. Continue for 3 miles, driving north. River Road merges into 97th Avenue N for 0.2 mile before you turn right onto Russell Avenue N. The entrance to Coon Rapids Dam Regional Park will be on your right in 1 mile. GPS: N45°08.43167' / W93°18.77333'

River Overview

The Mississippi River is one of the most famous rivers in the United States with some rankings marking it as the fourth longest and the second largest watershed in the world. That might sound intimidating, but this section of the "Mighty Mississippi" is far more tranquil than its nickname might lead you to believe. The river between Coon Rapids Dam and Psycho Suzi's has an industrial vibe, evident by the various buildings (some decaying, some not) and power plants along the shore. Coon Rapids Dam itself is the head of navigation, meaning it's the farthest point above the mouth of the river that's navigable by ships.

The Paddle

I met up with Sara and Michael (or "Westy," as Sara called him) on Psycho Suzi's patio for our second group paddle. We set off for Coon Rapids Dam Regional Park.

The put-in at Coon Rapids is easy to find from the parking lot: you'll move your boards (or whatever your paddling preference) across a pavilion (where you might see some summer grills fired up) and down to the eastern shore of the Mississippi along a thin slice of sandy beach. You won't start a beach volleyball game here anytime soon, but there's plenty of space to launch.

From the launch, we turned left to start our paddle south down the Mississippi River. Coincidentally we kept left for the entire paddle as we passed various islands along the way, such as Banfill Island and Durnam Island. That said, there's no danger in going around the islands as you see fit.

Early on, from the launch and for a considerable portion of the paddle, it was easy to forget that I was on the Mighty Mississippi itself. The water was running just as flat as its tributary, the Minnesota River, but, of course, it's all subject to the weather. Both Westy and Sara had previously done the same run on the Mississippi, completing it almost an hour faster than we would, thanks to a steady current. On this day, however, we only briefly hit a top speed of about 7.7 miles per hour. Our average came out to a more modest 4.4.

The Mississippi, as one can imagine, is also a respectably wide river. For a paddler, that means it's easy to tackle what small rapids do come up and just as easy to avoid them if you're on a stand-up paddleboard and would rather not risk

Getting ready to push off onto the Mississippi River at Coon Rapids Dam Regional Park JOE BAUR

dipping into the river, which was unfortunately rather brown thanks to some recent storms. I, for one, was happy to keep afloat and avoid the cool dip despite the hot sun bouncing off my SPF 50 sunblocked skin.

At the halfway point, wedged comfortably between Durnam Island to the west and Anoka County Riverfront Park to the east, the three of us paused to share a can of Mexican Honey Imperial Lager from Minneapolis's own Indeed Brewing Company. It's also around this point that the scenic Minneapolis skyline starts to poke above the horizon. So there I was, floating on the Mississippi, feeling like I was in the middle of a remote national park but with one of my favorite cities in the world just in sight, all while being refreshed by a local beer and amused by good company.

All I could think was, "This does not suck."

The second half went by considerably quickly as we paddled underneath I-694 and onward to the Lowry Bridge—a favorite of local Instagramers. If you time your paddle right and arrive after sunset, you can get some great shots of the bridge lit up. Of course you don't want to paddle too late and be caught dangerously paddling in the dark. I was happy enough to shoot the bridge with the sun still peeking out over the horizon.

Mississippi River

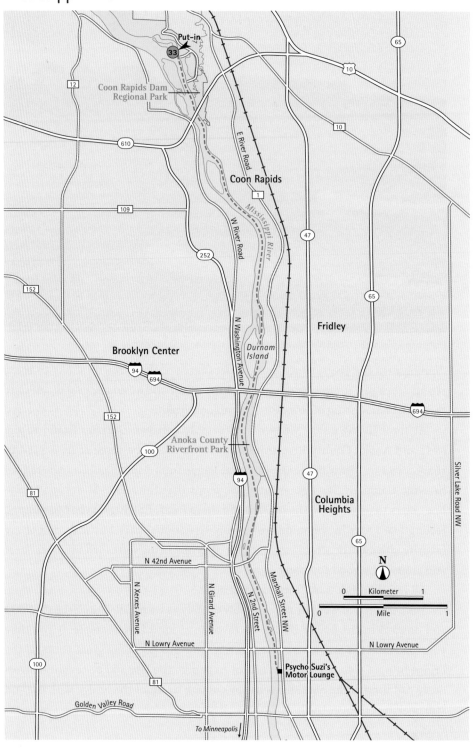

A PRIMER ON THE MISSISSIPPI

We've all heard about the Mississippi River. Maybe you're even one of the few Americans who *aren't* geographically challenged and you have a general idea of where it runs. Whatever the case may be, it's probably safe to assume you could use a primer—just as I needed before writing this book.

Remember how the Minnesota River was historically the much larger Glacial River Warren during the last ice age? And remember how the Minnesota River is now a tributary of the Mississippi? Well, 12,000 years ago, the roles were reversed. The Mighty Mississippi was a mere tributary to the Glacial River Warren that later became the Minnesota River.

Now hold onto your hats, geology nerds, because the Saint Peter Sandstone (in time) gave way to rushing waters. However, the Platteville Limestone (full of fossils) above the Saint Peter Sandstone was more resistant. Over time, this led to what is now the only naturally formed falls on the whole of the Mississippi River, and Native Americans of the area revered it.

Today, it's known as Saint Anthony Falls and can still be seen near today's downtown Minneapolis.

You should reach Lowry Avenue Bridge at about the 9.6-mile marker. That means you have almost 0.5 mile to get yourself over to the eastern edge of the Mississippi River and make sure you don't miss the dock up to Psycho Suzi's. It's very noticeable. You might even have a chance to ruin a couple's romantic moment as they watch the sunset on the dock. But I suppose it is possible for truly oblivious paddlers to miss it.

Once you reach the dock and shore at the 10-mile marker, you'll carry your gear up a steep, paved path that leads right up to Psycho Suzi's where you're more than welcome to enjoy that nightcap you've earned.

Paddle Information

Organization: Fort Snelling State Park, 101 Snelling Lake Rd., Saint Paul; (612) 279-3550; www.dnr.state.mn.us/state_parks/fort_snelling/index.html

Contact/outfitter: Silver Creek Paddle, 610 S.E. 9th St., Minneapolis; (612) 206-1469; silvercreekpaddle.com

34 Lake Nokomis

Lake Nokomis is anchored on the southern edge of Minneapolis's Grand Round and makes for a perfect introductory paddle. While everyone's over at the Chain of Lakes, you can mellow out a bit at Lake Nokomis to get your feet wet (pun intended) with your paddle of choice. Rentals are available, and there's a small beach where you can relax following the paddle.

Start/End: Lake Nokomis Main Beach
N 44 54' 43.3" / W93 14' 33.1"
Distance: 2 miles
Float time: About 40 minutes
Difficulty rating: Easy
Nearest city/town: Minneapolis
Boats used: Pedal boat, kayak, canoe, stand-up paddleboard
Getting there: From Minneapolis, take I-35 W south to exit 13 toward 46th Street. Merge onto Stevens Avenue southward, turn left onto E. 46th Street, and continue for 1.4 miles. Turn right onto Cedar Avenue S for 0.8 mile and then take a sharp left onto W. Lake Nokomis Parkway. The parking lot will be on your right in 0.3 mile.

From Saint Paul, take US 52 S to MN 110 W. After about 5 miles on MN 110 W, get on MN 55 W then MN 62 toward Cedar Avenue in Minneapolis. Take the Cedar Avenue exit in 4.3 miles. Turn northward onto Cedar Avenue S for 0.7 mile and turn right onto W. Lake Nokomis Parkway. The parking lot will be on your right in 0.3 mile. GPS: N44°54.72167' / W93°14.55167'

Lake Overview

Lake Nokomis is one of several lakes within Minneapolis's city limits. Like some of the other lakes in the area, Nokomis was dredged after being purchased in 1907 to turn the former marshland into the lake we see today.

Of course that doesn't mean the city is settling. Over recent years, the lake has been the subject of various preservation projects to harvest native vegetation around Nokomis's shores. Besides paddling, it's a popular spot for fishing, relaxing on the sand, and walking, and cyclists might recognize the area from the Minneapolis Grand Round ride.

Sara floats under Cedar Avenue on Lake Nokomis. JOE BAUR

Swimming is another popular activity in the lake. It should be noted that there is a sudden drop with the lake bed, which contributed to a tragic drowning in 2006. So if you go swimming after the paddle, stay within the designated area.

The Paddle

Lake Nokomis is where I probably should have begun. Why? Simply put, it's an easy paddle. Experienced paddlers might honestly find themselves a tad bored here, but newbies or those who have been off the water for several months would be smart to use Nokomis as a quick refresher course. However, even skilled, adventure-seeking paddlers admit that Nokomis is a relaxing option for an easy weekday paddle right in the city. The Twin Cities are blessed with lakes, and they sure make use of them.

The natural launch point for Nokomis is right on the main beach, though there's also the 50th Street Beach on the eastern edge. From the main beach, Sara (paddling with me once again) and I opted to paddle the lake clockwise only because of the way the wind was blowing. You're welcome to lick your finger, stick it in the air, and figure out your own direction.

FROM AMELIA TO NOKOMIS

Lake Nokomis didn't always go by "Nokomis." The lake was first called Lake Amelia in the early nineteenth century in a nod to Capt. George Gooding's daughter of the same name. But by 1910, the lake took a turn back to its indigenous roots. After all, the body of water was there before Mr. Gooding and his daughter came around.

Its current name, Nokomis, is in honor of the grandmother of Hiawatha, who herself was a Native American hero in Henry Wadsworth Longfellow's poem, *The Song of Hiawatha*. (In traditional Ojibwa stories, Nokomis is also the name of the grandmother of the spirit Nanabozho.)

In the poem, Nokomis has a daughter named Wenonah. Nokomis, being the wise mother that she is, discourages Wenonah from being seduced by Mudjekeewis. Turns out, Nokomis was right about Mudjekeewis, who left Wenonah, and she died in childbirth. Nokomis then stepped up to the plate to raise baby Hiawatha herself: "The wrinkled old Nokomis / Nursed the little Hiawatha."

Nokomis also translates to "my grandmother."

Given its size and the agreeable summer weather, Nokomis was a breeze. Sara and I meandered along the shores of Nokomis with ease. She even took a couple of work calls as we continued along our way in the late morning hours.

At 1.2 miles, we dipped underneath Cedar Avenue briefly before making our turn back northeast toward the main beach. In retrospect the paddle would have been a little longer had we truly hugged the shore, which is why I opted to call this a 2-mile paddle instead of the 1.9 miles I actually recorded. We missed a small chunk of the southern end of the lake, opting to follow the wind as it pushed us under the bridge.

Then again, that's the beauty of lake paddles. You can do with it what you will. They're like the water equivalents of high school tracks. Some will show up, ready to do some sprints. Others will take in a light jog. Nokomis is perfect for all of the above. Paddlers in training can find plenty of space to work on creating powerful strokes, whereas true beginners can rest easy knowing that they're likely to find considerably flat water here to practice on. Had Sara and I been true beginners, there'd be little embarrassment or danger if either one of us fell in before ending our paddle back at the main beach.

Lake Nokomis

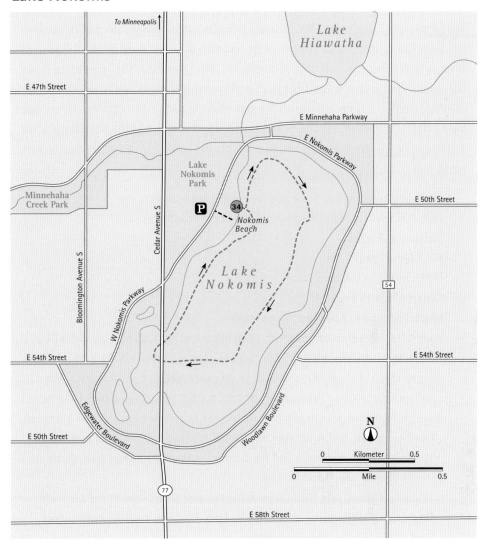

Paddle Information

Organization: Minneapolis Park & Recreation Board, 2117 W. River Rd., Minneapolis; (612) 230-6400; minneapolisparks.org

Contacts/outfitters: Silver Creek Paddle, 610 S.E. 9th St., Minneapolis; (612) 206-1469; silvercreekpaddle.com

Wheel Fun Rentals, 5022 W. Lake Nokomis Pkwy., Minneapolis; (877) 273-2453; wheel funrentals.com

35 Minnesota River

The Minnesota River makes for a natural choice when considering paddles within the Twin Cities metro area thanks to its location as a tributary of the Mississippi River, which flows through both Minneapolis and Saint Paul. The Minnesota flows northwest right into the Mississippi at a point where you're in the middle of the southern border of both city limits. For this relaxing paddle through the Minnesota Valley National Wildlife Refuge, however, we stop just short of the Mississippi after paddling a hair under 9 miles, starting underneath I-35W from a nondescript launch point.

Start: Southwest end of Black Dog Lake under the I-35 W bridge

End: Fort Snelling State Park, 101 Snelling Lake Road, Saint Paul

Distance: 8.8 miles

Float time: About 2 hours

Difficulty rating: Moderate due to distance

Current: Slow to moderate

Nearest city/town: Saint Paul, Bloomington

Boats used: Canoe, kayak, johnboat, small motorized craft, stand-up paddleboard

Getting there: To takeout: From Minneapolis, take I-35 W south for 3.8 miles. Stay in one of the three right-hand lanes to turn onto MN 62 E for 4.7 miles. MN 62E merges with MN 55. Continue on MN 55 E for 0.6 mile. Stay in one of the two right lanes to merge onto MN 5 W toward the airport and continue for 1.6 miles. Take the exit for Post Road; turn left. Continue about 1.3 miles and turn right. Stay to the right, and you'll find the takeout on the right shortly after that turn, almost directly underneath MN 55.

From Saint Paul, take US 52 S for 5.4 miles. Exit onto I-494 W for 7.9 miles. Then, at exit 1A&B merge onto MN 5 E. After 1.5 miles, take the exit for Post Road and follow the directions above.

To put-in from takeout: Backtrack on Post Road to MN 5 W and drive for 0.8 mile. Merge onto I-494 W/MN 5 W and continue for 1.6 miles. Take exit 2C toward MN 77 S. Stay in the left lane toward Killebrew Drive. Stay left again for MN 77 S and continue for 1 mile. Take the CR 1/Old Shakopee Road exit and drive for 0.3 mile. Turn right toward E. Old Shakopee Road for 2 miles. Continue to Nicollet Avenue S, W. 102nd Street, and Lyndale Avenue S toward the parking lot right on the Minnesota River and practically underneath I-35 W. GPS: N44°48.06333' / W93°17.31833'

River Overview

As we've already noted, the Minnesota River is a tributary of the Mississippi River, stretching some 332 miles across the state of Minnesota before dumping into the Mississippi near the heart of the Twin Cities. This paddle goes through the Minnesota Valley National Wildlife Refuge, which is one of only four of its kind in an American urban area—and the largest. The valley is approximately 5 miles wide and 250 feet deep, carved into the earth (like most of Minnesota's waters) by massive glacial currents. The Minnesota River can specifically trace its history back to the prehistoric Glacial River Warren around 10,000 years ago at the end of the last North American ice age. Both the Minnesota Territory and the state were named after the river.

The Cedar Avenue Bridge over the Minnesota River gets the Instagram treatment. JOE BAUR

The Paddle

I met Michael (or "Westy," as Sara called him) at the Fort Snelling train station at the edge of Minneapolis, where he picked me up in a large vehicle with a trailer attached and his paddleboard secured. We exchanged the usual cordial introductions and commenced with the standard chit-chat: "Where are you from? What do you do? What're you doing up here?"

Before long we arrived at Fort Snelling State Park, where we would leave Westy's vehicle to shuttle back at the end of the paddle. Sara got a bit lost trying to find the parking lot underneath the Mendota Bridge. It is indeed a bit tricky, but there are signs noting the "boat landing" along the way—not to mention the river is always a good indicator of where you need to go.

Once Sara arrived, we grabbed and secured her boards, and made south for our launch point underneath I-35 W in Bloomington, Minnesota. The launch point slopes conveniently right into the water, which makes for an easy drop-off as far as the boards are concerned, though we did notice one overly ambitious gentleman almost lose his speedboat after attempting to back his truck into the river, untie his boat, and drive off with some odd hope that the boat would stay in place. Had Sara not stepped in to offer to hold on to the rope attached to the boat, I'd have a much more comical intro to this paddle.

CANNING MINNESOTA

The Minnesota River played an important commercial role in the history of the Twin Cities. Historically, Minnesota was known for its canning industry (think food preservation), and the Minnesota River was at the heart of it all. Familiar with Green Giant and its *jolly* logo? The company traces its roots back to the Minnesota Valley Canning Company.

The river also became one of the nation's largest producers of sweet corn near the middle of the twentieth century. Eventually the company was acquired by General Mills (founded in Minneapolis and still headquartered in a western suburb). While times have changed for the canning industry, the Minnesota River continues to move barges of farm grains to the respective ports of Minneapolis and Saint Paul before they are shipped down the Mississippi River.

I couldn't believe it at the time, but it had been about six months since my last paddle. It was off the coast of Mexico's Baja Peninsula, and choppy waters kept me from gaining any serious miles. This time, though, there was no turning back. I had a book to write, after all.

Luckily the conditions were perfect for someone looking to get their sea legs back. The Minnesota River is plenty wide, so that alleviated any concern of navigating narrow channels. And there was little wind to speak of. At our fastest, we hit about 7.5 miles per hour, but averaged somewhere closer to 4.5. Of course, I take full responsibility for the slow start. It never ceases to amaze me how quickly our muscles forget how to do seemingly basic tasks, like standing on a board without falling. (For the record, I did not fall.)

We were also fortunate to have packed for the environment. Before heading out, I wondered aloud if I should bring my bug spray, at which point my sister-in-law reminded me that she and my brother were running from clouds of mosquitoes while hiking at Fort Snelling the summer before. If you're paddling in the Twin Cities' humid summer months, bug spray is a necessity, especially on the Minnesota River.

Amazingly, there's not much traffic on the Minnesota, something Westy remarked upon a number of times. Besides the aforementioned speedboat, there wasn't any other water traffic the entire paddle. There were some wildlife and families occasionally popping up along the shore, but for all intents and purposes, the river was ours for those two evening hours floating on the Minnesota River. It again reminded me why the Twin Cities make for the perfect environment for anyone looking to get a mix of nature and urbanity.

While most of the paddle felt like a remote river, reminders of city life occasionally came and went. There's the Cedar Avenue Bridge 3.5 miles into the hike, followed by a constant hum of airplanes landing for almost the entirety of the second half of the paddle. Minneapolis–Saint Paul International Airport is right next door to the river, after all, making for some great plane spotting for any aviation aficionados. We certainly slowed our paddle down to get a look at the belly of some of the planes passing by before continuing on until the takeout on the left and just under Mendota Bridge at 8.8 miles.

Minnesota River

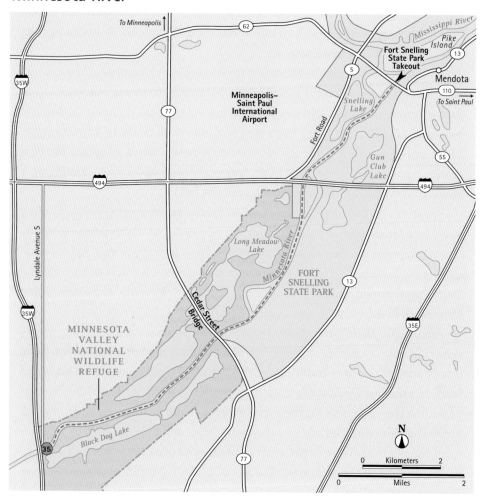

Paddle Information

Organization: Fort Snelling State Park, 101 Snelling Lake Rd., Saint Paul; (612) 279-3550; www.dnr.state.mn.us/state_parks/fort_snelling/index.html

Contact/outfitter: Silver Creek Paddle, 610 S.E. 9th St., Minneapolis; (612) 206-1469; silver creekpaddle.com

36 Long Lake

Paddling Long Lake in Ramsey County's Long Lake Regional Park takes you to more remote corners of the Twin Cities region for a peaceful, secluded paddle around 3.5 miles.

Start/End: Long Lake Public Beach

Distance: 3.5-mile loop

Float time: About 1 hour

Difficulty rating: Easy

Nearest city/town: New Brighton

Boats used: Canoe, kayak, small motorized craft, stand-up paddleboard

Getting there: Take I-35 north to MN 96 W. Turn left onto MN 96 W, followed quickly by a left onto Old Hwy. 8 NW. In 0.4 mile, turn right and follow the road until it ends at the parking lot. GPS: N45°04.47045' / W93°11.97280'

Lake Overview

Long Lake Regional Park offers a respite from the Twin Cities without having to plan a long drive or make hotel reservations. The park itself is known for its bur oak trees, some of which are more than 200 years old, surrounded by native prairie grass and the remnants of the farmsteads of decades past. You'll get a taste of it all on your paddle, but you'll especially notice some of the beautiful homes perched up along the shore.

The Paddle

The beauty of paddling Long Lake is that it feels remote without your actually having to glue yourself to the wheel for hours shelling out a hundred bucks on a hotel room. By car it's a mere 20 to 30 minutes outside of the Twin Cities—very accessible on a weekday, especially during those long summer nights when the sun feels like it'll never set.

Sara and I launched our stand-up paddleboards out of the Long Lake Public Beach, which requires a little walk from the parking lot. Ultimately it's nothing that'll put you on your back before you even get in the water, but it is long enough that you'll start to notice the weight of your board or kayak. In any event, once you launch, it's smooth sailing (or paddling) for the entire 3.5-mile loop.

This Long Lake view looks and feels more remote than it actually is. JOE BAUR

We opted to paddle clockwise, heading south from our launch. As always, we gauged how close we got to shore based on the amount of aquatic plants below and the depth of the water. After all, nothing slows up a paddle—especially on a paddleboard—like plants clinging to your fin and paddle. For the most part, however, Long Lake was relatively clear compared to other paddles, allowing us to hug closer to shore than usual.

At about 1.4 miles into the paddle, Long Lake narrows considerably. It's almost as if you're in a canal. This is when you really start to paddle close to some of the gorgeous homes on the shore. Of course, you can arrive here more quickly by heading north straight out of the launch.

With time to kill in our paddle, Sara made a quick pitch about including some information here on the importance of cleaning your boards or other watercraft after paddling. Invasive species are an issue in Minnesotan waters. You may even notice the agencies responsible for maintaining the respective waters dredging up invasive plants that have found their way where they don't belong. How do they get here? In short, people don't wash their boards, kayaks, or canoes. You paddle in one lake and then another without diligently ensuring that you've

Long Lake

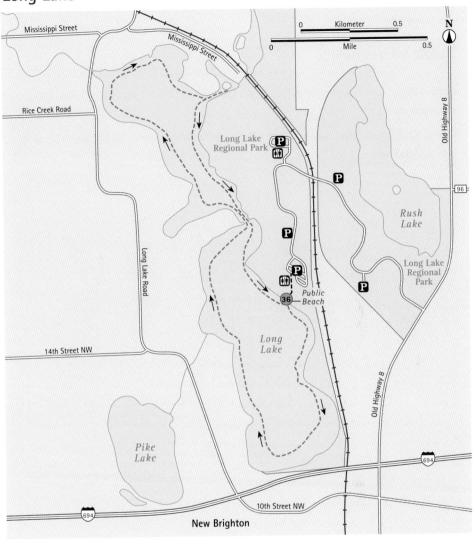

thoroughly cleaned your watercraft. The problem arises when you mistakenly transfer an invasive aquatic plant from one body of water to the next.

This came up because we had planned to move from Long Lake onto Lake Phalen later in the day. Luckily we were able to postpone cleaning, because Sara, being at the helm of Silver Creek Paddle, happens to have no shortage of boards, but we did make a point to switch out our gear, lest we serve as the engine that brings invasive species into a defenseless body of water. If you don't have the luxury of a trailer full of boards, then please make a point to clean up after yourself following every paddle.

Paddle Information

Organization: Long Lake Regional Park, 1500 Old Hwy. 8, New Brighton; (651) 748-2500; ramseycounty.us

Contact/outfitters: Silver Creek Paddle, 610 SE 9th St., Minneapolis; (612) 206-1469; silver creekpaddle.com

37 Lake Phalen

Saint Paul may not have the Chain of Lakes, but it does have Lake Phalen for those looking to keep east and enjoy the water. To its credit, it's a bit more quiet and serene for those who may find the Lake Calhoun side of things a tad overwhelming, especially in the thick of summer.

Start/End: Lake Phalen Boat Launch, 1600 Phalen Drive, Saint Paul

Distance: 2.6–mile loop

Float time: About 1 hour

Difficulty rating: Easy

Nearest city/town: Saint Paul

Boats used: Pedal boat, kayak, canoe, stand–up paddleboard

Getting there: From I-35E north of Saint Paul, take MN 36 east to US 61 S / Maplewood Drive. After about a mile, take a sharp left onto Frost Avenue. At the roundabout in 0.6 mile, take the first exit toward E. Shore Drive. Turn right to continue onto E. Shore Drive in 0.2 mile. Follow the road another 0.2 mile until it ends at the Lake Phalen Boat Launch. GPS: N44°59.64872' / W93°03.57655'

Lake Overview

Way back when, the city of Saint Paul bought Lake Phelan for a paltry $22,000. Of course the year was 1899, and things have changed a bit since then. What hasn't changed is that Phalen Regional Park has been open to the public since its creation. Like the other lakes in the metro region, Lake Phalen is an easy, flat paddle for those looking to get out and onto the water on a weekday after business hours. It's also a bit quieter than some of the other urban lakes included in this book.

The Paddle

Residents of Saint Paul are lucky to have Lake Phalen. If I were to be picky, I could complain about the overwhelming crowds that have the tendency to take over the Chain of Lakes in Minneapolis. Lake Phalen, however, remains blissfully serene for the most part, and that was certainly the case when Sara and I took our stand-up paddleboards to the Lake Phalen Boat Launch for an easy 2.6-mile paddle around the lake.

Lake Phalen is a typically quieter paddle than its Minneapolis siblings. JOE BAUR

Only two others were at the boat launch when we arrived—a couple of fishermen. Whenever you're carrying a stand-up paddleboard, it's not uncommon for passersby to ask about the board and what the paddling is like. "Is it hard? What does it feel like?" A paddleboard is like the toe shoes of the water, except stand-up paddleboarding is objectively cooler.

Right on cue, one of the fishermen asked us what stand-up paddleboarding is like, as we trotted down the dock with our boards under our arms. Here the dock dips nicely into the water, making for an easy stand-up paddleboard launch off to the side of the dock. After giving the boilerplate responses—"It's great! You should try it!"—Sara and I made our way south to start our loop around Lake Phalen.

Now I could lie and say there's something phenomenally interesting about Lake Phalen, but there isn't—at least to the general public. I mean, even the naming rights simply come from an early settler named Edward Phalen, who had made an early claim to some land around nearby Phalen Creek. It's not exactly heart-stopping history.

What makes Lake Phalen great is its reliability for folks living in or visiting Saint Paul. Get out of work early? Lake Phalen is there for a relaxing paddle. No

Lake Phalen

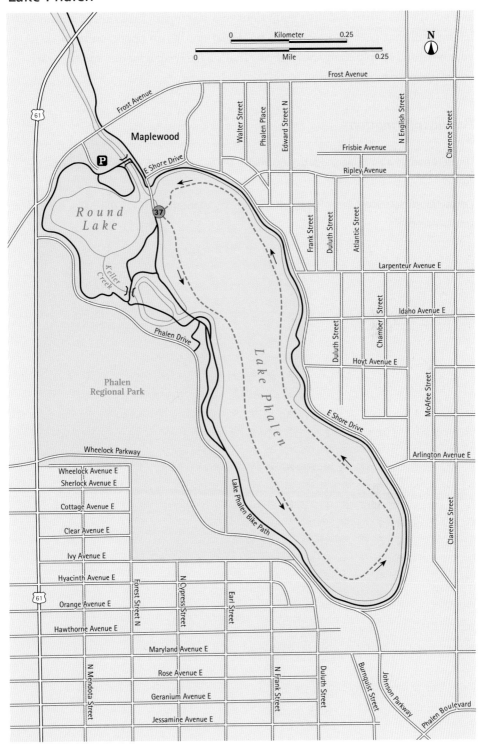

Frost Avenue

Frost Avenue

Maplewood

E Shore Drive

Walter Street

Phalen Place

Edward Street N

N English Street

Clarence Street

Frisbie Avenue

Ripley Avenue

Round Lake

37

Keller Creek

Frank Street

Duluth Street

Atlantic Street

Larpenteur Avenue E

Phalen Drive

Phalen Regional Park

Lake Phalen

Chamber Street

Idaho Avenue E

Duluth Street

Hoyt Avenue E

McAfee Street

E Shore Drive

Arlington Avenue E

Wheelock Parkway

Wheelock Avenue E

Sherlock Avenue E

Cottage Avenue E

Clear Avenue E

Ivy Avenue E

Hyacinth Avenue E

Orange Avenue E

Hawthorne Avenue E

Forest Street N

N Cypress Street

Earl Street

Lake Phalen Bike Path

Clarence Street

Maryland Avenue E

N Mendota Street

Rose Avenue E

Geranium Avenue E

Jessamine Avenue E

N Frank Street

Duluth Street

Burnquist Street

Johnson Parkway

Phalen Boulevard

0   Kilometer   0.25

0   Mile   0.25

N

need to think or worry too much about where you're heading, just hop on a board and go. It's the urban paddling equivalent of a metropark bike ride or a 3-mile hiking trail that goes in a loop with no deviation. It's an opportunity to clear your head and simply enjoy the fresh air. That's Lake Phalen for me, and there are worse places to be in the world.

Paddle Information

Organization: Phalen Regional Park, 1600 Phalen Dr., Saint Paul; (651) 266-6400; stpaul .gov

Contact/outfitter: Silver Creek Paddle, 610 SE 9th St., Minneapolis; (612) 206-1469; silver creekpaddle.com

38 Lake Calhoun to Lake of the Isles and Cedar Lake

The Chain of Lakes is a staple of Minneapolis and something any city the world over should envy. Here, you can hike, cycle, and paddle around three beautiful lakes, each with their own distinct vibe. Paddling yields yet another experience with the ability to float underneath bridges and through narrow canals that connect the lakes.

Start/End: Wheel Fun Rentals at Lake Calhoun, 3000 E. Calhoun Parkway, Minneapolis

Distance: 5.2 miles

Float time: About 2 hours

Difficulty rating: Easy

Nearest city/town: Minneapolis

Boats used: Canoe, pedal boat, kayak, canoe, stand-up paddleboard

Getting there: Take I-94 west to exit 231B toward Hennepin Avenue; keep left and follow signs for Hennepin Avenue. After about 1 mile on Hennepin Avenue S, turn right onto Lagoon Avenue, followed shortly thereafter by a left onto E. Calhoun Parkway. The launch at Wheel Fun Rentals will be on your right. GPS: N44°56.91258' / W93°18.397'

Lake Overview

The Chain of Lakes—comprising Lake Calhoun, Lake of the Isles, and Cedar Lake—is arguably the natural crown jewel of Minneapolis. This paddle focuses on the latter two lakes, with Lake of the Isles boasting a high level of water clarity, revealing a number of aquatic plants, and Cedar Lake offering some of the best views of the Minneapolis skyline.

The Paddle

I debated putting this into the book. We already have an urban hike and bike ride that take you around the Chain of Lakes, leaving me to wonder if a paddle was really necessary. Then I decided I was foolish for thinking such silly thoughts. How could the Chain of Lakes *not* be included in the region's best paddles? Considering the number of small vessels you'll see out on the Chain of Lakes at

Drifting between Lake of the Isles and Cedar Lake—a view only possible by water JOE BAUR

any given time—save winter—it indeed is a popular way to spend a weekend afternoon.

This time I opted to rent a kayak from Wheel Fun Rentals. Of course you can bring your own kayak or stand-up paddleboard, but this is how most residents and visitors enjoy the lake. I was also accompanied by my friend Alicia, a fellow travel writer based out of Fargo, North Dakota, who happened to be in the area.

Wheel Fun Rentals is housed in an unmistakable little shack in the northeastern corner of Lake Calhoun, right off its bike trail and next to the Tin Fish eatery. Alicia and I launched from the northeastern shore and made a hard right for the canal leading north up to the Lake of the Isles. While you're welcome to paddle around Lake Calhoun, it's about 3 miles in perimeter and less exciting to tackle in the water than by foot or bike. So for the purposes of the paddle and coming up with a different experience, Lake Calhoun only served as our point of launch.

Less than 0.1 mile into the paddle, you're already getting a different view of the Chain of Lakes as you float down the canal leading between Lake Calhoun and Lake of the Isles. After passing the first bridge, the water opens up a bit wider than that of the canal, but this isn't Lake of the Isles. You'll quickly float

Lake Calhoun to Lake of the Isles and Cedar Lake

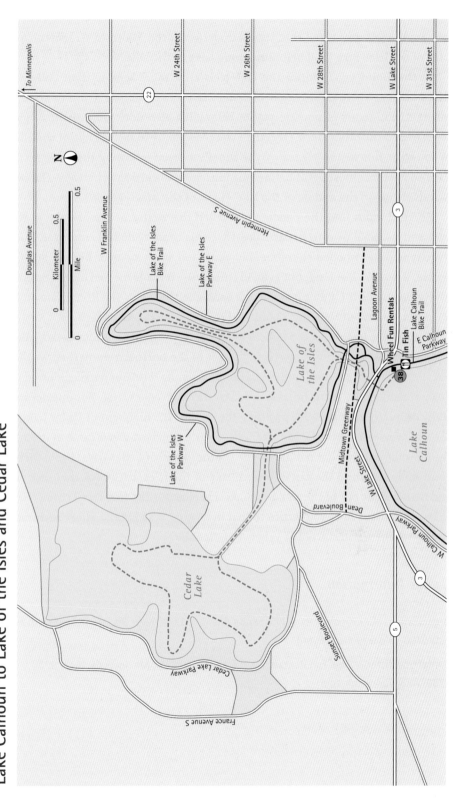

into another narrow canal that crawls underneath the Midtown Greenway and Lake of the Isles Bike Trail before reaching Lake of the Isles.

At this point you'll notice the lake feels a bit more remote than Calhoun. That's because there's quite a bit of water clarity here, allowing you to see the substantial amount of aquatic plants below. It's also noticeably shallow here compared to the other lakes. Of course you're welcome to tackle Lake of the Isles as you wish, but we mostly traced the shoreline, even following the water to its narrow, northernmost point before turning back and cutting in between the two islands sitting in the middle of the lake. (Lake of the *Isles*—get it?)

About 2 miles into the paddle we reached the western edge of Lake of the Isles and its canal over to Cedar Lake. Now this canal truly feels removed from the city with its wooded shoreline, lily pads, and scant signs of human life. Of course, it doesn't last long, but even in its brevity, it made me feel like I'd be positively ridiculous if I didn't include this paddle in the book. The Ron Swanson in me could see myself bringing a book and resting in that canal a bit.

The canal is just under 0.5 mile in length before it pours out into Cedar Lake. You can paddle more miles by staying closer to the northern shore than we did, but the shallow shores and numerous plants latching onto our paddles slowed us down considerably. We ultimately opted to stay in deeper water. But one doesn't really come to Cedar Lake for paddling the shores. The highlight of Cedar Lake is the view you can get of the Minneapolis skyline. The best views came at around the 3.8-mile point of our paddle on the southern end of Cedar Lake. From there, you simply return to the canal toward Lake of the Isles, backtrack that section, and hang a right out of the canal to make a beeline for the first canal connecting to Lake Calhoun. Once you return to that first canal, it's a simple, short backtrack paddle to where you started at Wheel Fun Rentals.

Paddle Information

Organization: Minneapolis Park & Recreation Board, 2117 W. River Rd., Minneapolis; (612) 230-6400; minneapolisparks.org

Contact/outfitter: Wheel Fun Rentals, 3000 E. Calhoun Pkwy., Minneapolis; (612) 823-5765; wheelfunrentals.com

39 White Bear Lake

Both White Bear Lakes, the body of water and the adjacent town of the same name, are popular weekend destinations for Twin Cities residents looking for a respite from city life. The paddle takes you around considerable boat traffic to diverse corners of the lake, from wealthy residential estates to a more wild corner full of cottonwoods and reeds.

> Start/End: Tally's Dockside, 4441 Lake Ave S, Saint Paul
>
> Distance: 6.5 miles
>
> Float time: About 2.5 hours
>
> Difficulty rating: Moderate due to distance
>
> Nearest city/town: White Bear Lake
>
> Boats used: Canoe, kayak, small motorized craft, jet skis, pontoons
>
> Getting there: Take US 61 north toward White Bear Avenue in White Bear Lake, Minnesota. Turn right onto White Bear Avenue, followed by a left onto Lake Avenue S in 0.2 mile, then another quick left to stay on Lake Avenue S. Tally's Dockside will be on the right in 0.1 mile. GPS: N45°04.54562' / W93°00.98355'

Lake Overview

The lake at White Bear Lake became a popular resort area, attracting travelers from across the Mississippi River in the late nineteenth century. People traveled by steamboat and train to get to the hotels that lined the shores, taking in the restaurants, theaters, and shops set up downtown during their stay. The resort era faded away in the early twentieth century, but the lake has been a constant. Today, White Bear Lake is a popular destination for paddlers with up to 2,416 acres to explore and enjoy.

The Paddle

From Tally's Dockside, you set out among a variety of motorized boats and Jet Skis. Besides kayaks, you can rent canoes and pontoons, so the area can be busy. Because of all the traffic, it's not a preferred area for stand-up paddleboarders; a kayak is a much more suitable option in these parts. Even in the middle of the week, there can be considerable activity. It's also not a paddle for bashful

Kayaking is the way to tackle White Bear Lake. ALICIA UNDERLEE NELSON

individuals, because the diners at nearby Tally's BBQ Restaurant and Bar will definitely keep an eye on you as you hop into the kayak.

Paddling counterclockwise around the lake, you can't get too close to the shore on the southern end or you'll run into the docks. So be smart and keep your distance. Some of the docks out here are surprisingly long for a residential area, almost as long as piers, even. They're long, because—as you'll see—the lake is very shallow along the southern edge. Water markers point out the truly shallow areas and the occasional submerged sandbar or rock that could cause you trouble. When we did this paddle in 2016, the water was only 3 or 4 feet deep.

White Bear Lake is not a poor area, and that's obvious from the residences surrounding the lake. It's pure upper class out here—large houses with backyards to match and multiple boats to cap off a collection of expensive toys. Things calm down a bit toward the Bellaire area, another residential area along the lake. There's also a public beach that you can spot from the water.

The eastern side of the lake dips into Mahtomedi, which is largely more of what you saw before. There are houses, docks, and, yes, shallow water. On my paddle there seemed to be more fishermen in this corner of the lake than in others.

Then, the estates manage to grow even larger as you continue north toward Dellwood. But you'll likely have to skip the northern end of the lake if there's

WHITE BEAR LAKE

The origins of White Bear Lake are steeped in American legend. Mrs. Carl T. Thayer writes in her book *Indian Legends of Minnesota*:

> It is said that a Sioux maiden fell in love with a Chippewa brave. She, the daughter of the Chief, on learning that her father planned war against the Chippewa, ran to her lover and warned him. The brave went alone into the Sioux village to ask for peace and the hand of the maiden. Before the Chief would agree, the Chippewa would have to do a brave deed.
>
> The lovers usually met on Manitou Island. One day, as the brave approached the Island, anticipating a meeting with his beloved, he saw, to his horror, a great white bear attacking her. He dashed to her rescue. Freed, she ran to get help from her father and the other Sioux. Returning, they saw the brave sink his knife into the bear. But too late, they both fell to the ground dead. Slowly, as they watched, the spirits of the brave and the bear rose from their prone bodies. It is said that even today, as night falls, the spirits of the bear and the brave wander the Island eternally in search of each other.

Mark Twain's version, however, from *Life on the Mississippi* invokes the "White Bear" with a different ending to the story:

> The animal turned, and with one stroke of his huge paw brought the lovers heart to heart, but the next moment the warrior, with one plunge of the blade of his knife, opened the crimson sluices of death, and the dying bear relaxed his hold. That night, there was no more sleep for the band or the lovers, and as the young and the old danced about the carcass of the dead monster, the gallant warrior was presented with another plume, and ere another moon had set he had a living treasure added to his heart. Their children for many years played upon the skin of the white bear—from which the lake derives its name, and the maiden and the brave remembered long the fearful scene and rescue that made them one, for Kis-se-me-pa and Ka-go-ga could never forget their fearful encounter with the huge monster that came so near sending them to the happy hunting ground.

White Bear Lake

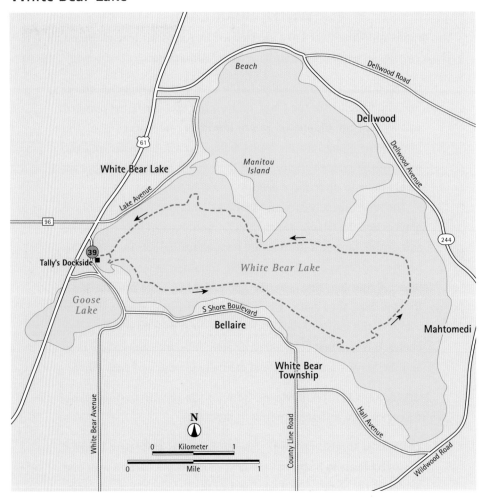

significant boat traffic. The area gets narrow, and it can be a bit dangerous to continue in your kayak. Instead, continue west toward the peninsula that juts out between the northern and western ends of the lake. Things take a turn for the wild side here. There are fewer docks, and what dwellings do exist are farther from the shore. Cottonwoods and reeds are plentiful here, with water lilies seemingly everywhere. If you could press Pause for a moment, you might be able to hear nearby ducks and geese passing the day in the reeds.

There are more rocks and shallow water to avoid here, but nearly everything is marked to a comical extent with buoys. You'd have to be extremely lost in the moment to actually hit something by surprise.

White Bear Lake sparkles on a sunny afternoon kayak. ALICIA UNDERLEE NELSON

Paddle Information

Organization: White Bear Lake County Park, 5050 Lake Avenue, White Bear Lake; (651) 748-2500; parks.co.ramsey.mn.us

Contact/outfitter: Tally's Dockside, 4440 Lake Ave. S, White Bear Lake; (651) 429-2633; https://cghooks.com

40 Saint Croix River

The Saint Croix runs smoothly up here on the Minnesota-Wisconsin border. Over 10 miles of paddling (or floating along the stream), you'll see wildlife and pristine, green surroundings as you skate along the river between tiny historic town of Marine on Saint Croix and Stillwater, Minnesota.

Start: Behind the Marine General Store, 101 Judd Street, Marine on Saint Croix

End: Saint Croix River Public Boat Ramp, Stillwater

Distance: 10.3 miles

Float time: About 3 hours

Difficulty rating: Medium due to length

Nearest city/town: Marine on Saint Croix, Stillwater

Boats used: Canoe, kayak, small motorized craft, stand-up paddleboard

Getting there: To takeout: From Saint Paul, take I-94 to I-694; continue for about 5.5 miles to exit 52B for MN 36 E toward Stillwater. After about 5 miles on MN 36 E, stay in one of the two left-hand lanes to turn toward Manning Avenue N. In 3 miles, turn right onto MN 96 E/Dellwood Road. After about 2.8 miles, turn left to MN 95N/Main Street N/Saint Croix Trail. In 0.6 mile, turn right and follow the road to the Saint Croix River Public Boat Ramp. GPS: N45 4' 49.112" / W92 18' 1.161"

To put-in from takeout: Drive north on MN 95 N/Saint Croix Trail for about 9.5 miles. Turn right onto Maple Street and park behind the Marine General Store at Judd and Maple Streets. A footpath behind the store leads to the put-in. GPS: N45°11.92120' / W92°46.14997'

River Overview

The Saint Croix River is a tributary of the Mississippi River and was one of the first eight rivers to receive protection by the National Wild and Scenic Rivers Act of 1968. It's a free-flowing river that's only interrupted once—by a hydroelectric dam operated by the Northern States Power Company at Saint Croix Falls, Wisconsin. Its name comes from Jean-Baptiste-Louis Franquelin and his late seventeenth-century map that noted a "Fort St. Croix" along the river. Thus, it received the French name Rivière de Sainte-Croix. Of course, the French weren't the first ones there. The Sioux referred to it as the Ouasisacadeba, according to one French document, as well as the more simple Ouadeba. The latter word represents the Dakota word *watpá* meaning "river." The Ojibwa, too, had their own names for the river throughout their history with the waterway.

The Paddle

Marine on Saint Croix is a tiny town of just under 700 residents that dates back to the mid-nineteenth century, when it was Marine Mills. According to the city of Marine on Saint Croix, it was the site of the first commercial sawmill. Considering that history, it's no surprise that much of the city finds itself listed on the National Register of Historic Places. The 450-acre historic district received the honor in 1974 for its significance in architecture and early American exploration and settlement, as well as industry. Immigration played an important role in the town's early days, notably from the Swedish working class.

The main reason to come here is for a paddle on the Saint Croix River, an official National Scenic Riverway that falls under the protection of the National Park Service. As a tributary of the mighty Mississippi River that cuts through the Twin Cities, the Saint Croix rises in northwestern Wisconsin and flows southwest to

Taking a break on the gentle Saint Croix CALLIE R. WOLF

Getting ready to start the paddle down the Saint Croix CALLIE R. WOLF

the state border. In all it's about 169 miles long before its confluence with the Mississippi River.

For paddleboarders, this is St. Croix Stand Up Paddleboard Company territory, with their headquarters in Stillwater. To start this paddle, you'll park behind the Marine General Store at Maple and Judd Streets. There's a gravel trail behind the store that leads to the put-in. The current is very swift, so you'll be off as soon as you get in the water, which makes the stand-up paddleboard a great option.

The Saint Croix splits the states of Minnesota and Wisconsin. For the directionally challenged, everything on your left is Wisconsin, and Minnesota is on the right as you paddle or float south toward Stillwater, Minnesota. You'll notice a number of islands to navigate around along the river. This route has you stay to the right, but you can paddle as you like.

A high bridge marks the halfway point, an old piece of infrastructure that still serves as an active train route. Then you'll come across some pillars—remnants of an old bridge that hasn't fared as well as the rail bridge.

Wildlife is teeming throughout. There are eagles, cranes, and no shortage of hopping fish just to give you an idea. In all, it's a fast, scenic, and relaxing route

Saint Croix River

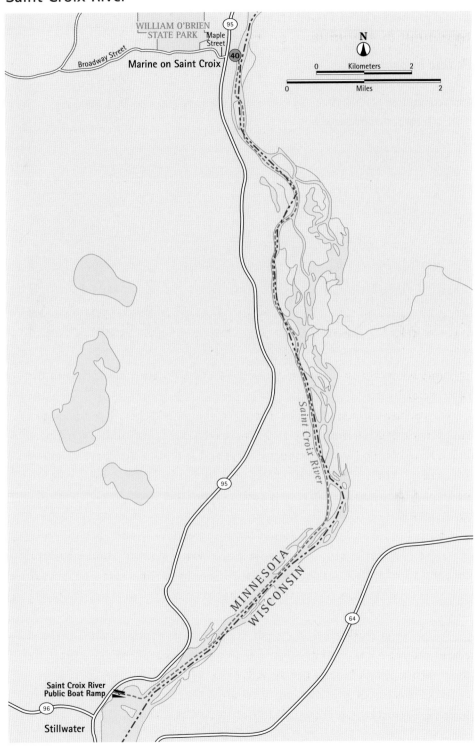

that gets you farther away from the Twin Cities than anything else in this book, should you need a bit of a respite from urbanity.

Paddle Information

Contact/outfitter: St. Croix Stand Up Paddleboard Company, 305 Alder St. E, Stillwater; (651) 271-1643; stcroixsupco.com

Adventure Index

(H) Hiking (MB) Mountain Biking (RC) Road Cycling (P) Paddling

About the Author

Joe Baur is a travel writer, filmmaker, and podcaster whose work has appeared in a variety of international publications from *BBC Travel* to *National Geographic*. Most recently he released *Talking Tico: (Mis)adventures of a Gringo In and Around Costa Rica* describing his year living and traveling in Central America (available at joebaur.com and Amazon). Currently he's based in Düsseldorf, Germany, and is continually trying to find his way off the tourist track.

About the Contributors

David Baur is a writer and author. He cowrote *Best Hikes Near Minneapolis and Saint Paul* with his brother, Joe, and his fiction has been featured in the anthology series *Robbed of Sleep*. He is still working to drag his first novel, *The Witches of Nicollet Island*, across the finish line. When not writing, he finds time for a day job as the Director of Communications at the Urban Land Institute Minnesota.

Steve Johnson is a self-propelled recreation junkie and fan of all things outdoors. A regular contributor to *Backpacker* and regional magazines across the country, some of Steve's other work includes *Minnesota Waterfalls*, *Loop Hikes Colorado*, and *Bicycling Wisconsin*. Steve lives with his family at a country place in southeastern Minnesota.